Mom's COMFORT FOOD

Desserts
Recipes

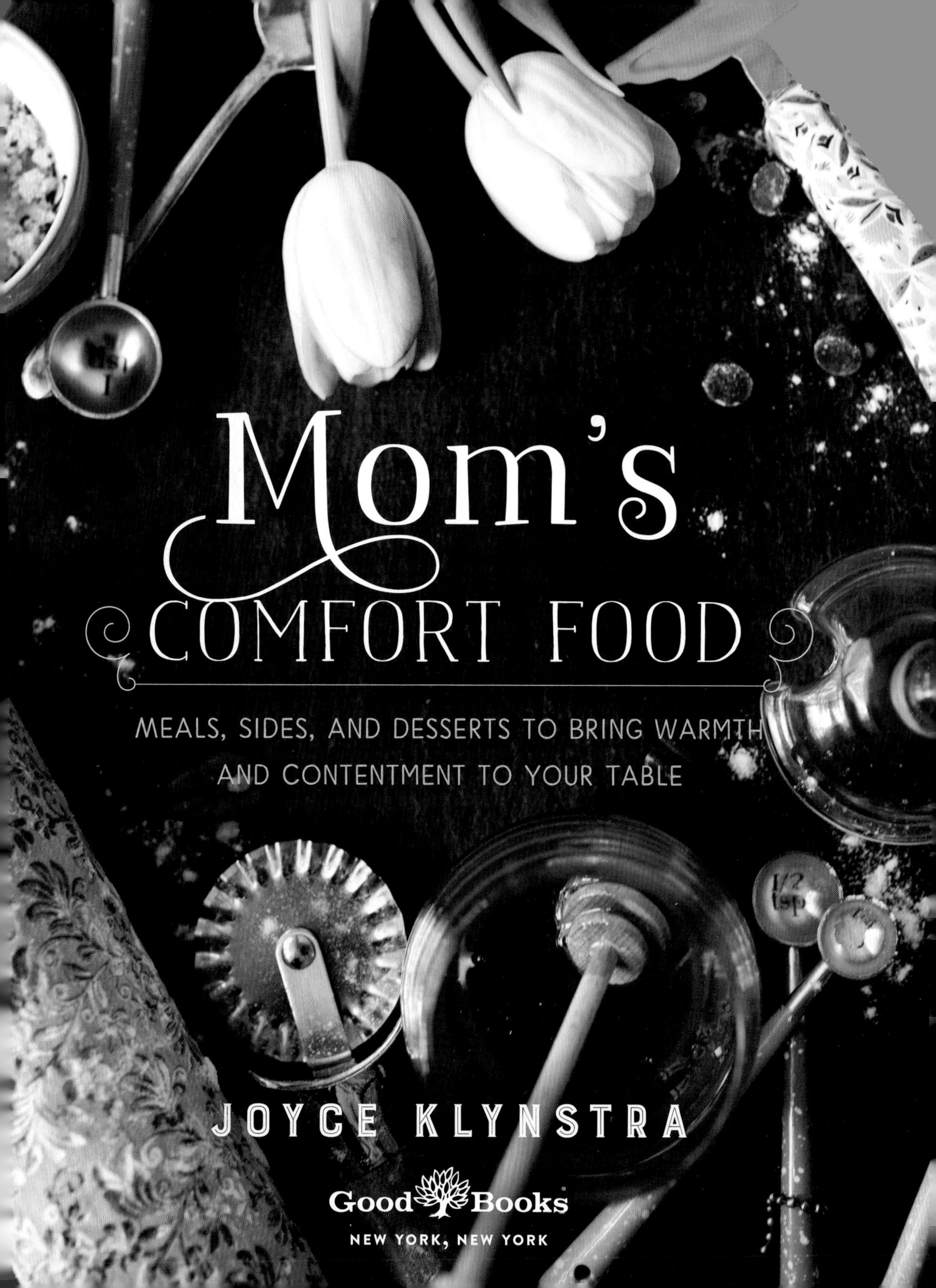

Mom's Comfort Food

Meals, Sides, and Desserts to Bring Warmth and Contentment to Your Table

Joyce Klynstra

Good Books
New York, New York

Good Books books may be purchased in bulk at special discounts for sales promotion, corporate gifts, fund-raising, or educational purposes. Special editions can also be created to specifications. For details, contact the Special Sales Department, Skyhorse Publishing, 307 West 36th Street, 11th Floor, New York, NY 10018 or info@skyhorsepublishing.com.

Good Books is an imprint of Skyhorse Publishing, Inc.®, a Delaware corporation.

Visit our website at www.skyhorsepublishing.com.

10 9 8 7 6 5 4 3 2

Library of Congress Cataloging-in-Publication Data is available on file.

Cover and interior design by Laura Klynstra
Cover and interior illustrations by Phil Rose, Shutterstock, and Maria B. Paints/Creative Market
Floral illustrations by Jung Suk Hyun/Shutterstock

Print ISBN: 978-1-68099-346-2
Ebook ISBN: 978-1-68099-389-9

Printed in China

FOR JIM

Miss you every day

Contents

Introduction 1

Favorites 2

APPETIZERS

Asian Meatballs 6

Bleu Cheese Artichoke Appetizer 8

Veggie Pizza 9

Chili con Queso 10

Joy's Olive Spread 13

Taco in the Round 14

Guacamole Dip 17

BREADS

Six-Week Bran Muffins 21

Banana Bread 22

Beer Bread 25

Easy Biscuits 26

Blueberry Muffins 29

Bread Machine Honey Oatmeal Bread 30

Zucchini Bread 33

BREAKFAST

Crustless Avocado Quiche 37

Baked French Toast 38

Breakfast Pizza 40

Buttermilk Pancakes with Blueberry Sauce 43

Pig in Blankets 45

Sausage Egg and Cheese Breakfast Braid 46

SOUPS

Dutch Pea Soup 50
Creamy Slow Cooker Potato Soup 51
Chicken Soup 54
Broccoli Soup 55
Vegetable Beef Soup 56
Butternut Squash Soup 59
Caledonia Band Booster Chili 60
Dutch Meatball Soup 63
Polish Kielbasa Slow Cooker Soup 64
Beef, Beer, and Barley Soup 65
Vegetable Cheese Soup 67
Potato Cheese Soup 69

MAIN DISHES

Wet Burritos 73
American Goulash 74
Swiss Cheese Chicken and Mushroom Bake 76
Chicken Pot Pie 79
Leah's Chicken Squares 80
Chicken Tater Tot Casserole 83
Tortilla Chicken Casserole 84
Corn Dogs 87
Creamed Asparagus on Biscuits 89
Creamed Chicken on Biscuits 90
Swedish Meatballs 91
Meat Loaf 92
Spaghetti Pie 95
Upside-Down Pizza 97

SALADS & SIDES

French Dressing 101
Strawberry Walnut Salad with Poppyseed Dressing 102
Make-Ahead Layered Chicken Salad 105
Pasta Asparagus Salad 107
Meme's M-50-Drive-In Potato Salad 108
Arborio Rice with Asparagus 110
BBQ Onions 113
Barb's Green Rice 115
Cauliflower & Cheese Sauce 116
Cheesy Potatoes 118
Slow Cooker Creamed Corn 119
Corn Cake 120
Honeyed Carrots 122
Green Beans 123
Refried Beans 124
Macaroni and Cheese 127

COOKIES & BARS

Aunt Margaret's Sugar Cookies 131

Ma's Chocolate Chip Cookies 132

Brownies 134

Rhubarb Bars 137

Dutch Butter Bars 138

Blonde Brownies 140

Almond Bars 143

CAKES

Apple Cake 146

Banana Cake 148

Carrot Pineapple Cake 151

Wedding Pound Cake 152

Decorator Frosting 154

Rum Cake 157

DESSERTS

Apple Crisp. 160

Dutch Apple Flat Pie 163

Fruit Pizza 164

Ice Cream Dessert 166

Chocolate Chip Cookie Dough Cheesecake 169

Oreo Cookie Dessert 170

Joan's Strawberry Shortcake 172

Karen's Strawberry Shortcake 175

Crunch Bar Ice Cream Dessert 176

Peach Enchiladas 179

PIES

Grammy Vonk's Pie Crust 183
No Roll Pie Crust 183
Cream Pie Four Ways 185
Dutch Apple Pie 186
Chocolate Chip Cookie Pie 189
Peach Pie 190
Pecan Joy Pie 193
Rhubarb Pie 194
Pumpkin Pie 197
Strawberry or Peach Pie 198

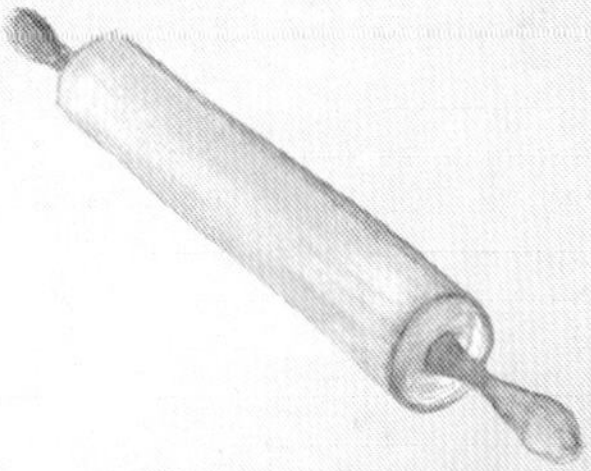

MERRY CHRISTMAS

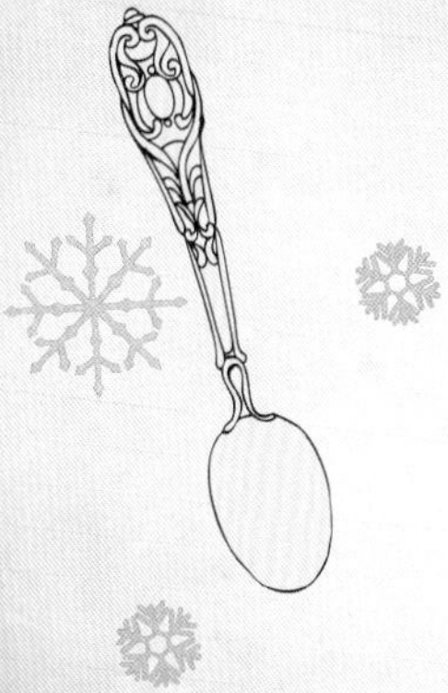

Brickle Graham Bites 203
Pecan Pie Bars 204
Fast and Easy Fudge 206
Graham Cracker Cookies 209
Peanut Butter Fudge 210
Kettle Corn 211
Party Mix 214
White Chocolate Party Mix 215
Peanut Brittle 217
Peanut Butter Balls 218

CANNING & FREEZING

How to Can 224
Burrito Sauce 225
Stewed Tomatoes 227
Sweet Zucchini Relish 230
Tomato Soup 231
Salsa 232
Applesauce 233
Freezer Corn 234
Freezer Strawberry Jam 236

Acknowledgments 238
Index 239
Conversion Chart 243
About the Author 244

The older I get, the more I realize
I just need the simple things in life:
A comfy home, good food on the table,
surrounded by
PEOPLE I LOVE.

50 Drive In
Open Dai A.M. — 11
Saturdays 8 A.M. — 9:30 P.M.
ALLENDALE, MICH.
Rice
Butter
pkg broccoli - chopped
onions
celery
1 Can jar Cheese Whiz
Cream
mush.
Mix together above ingredients
Bake at 350°
for 35 min
uncovered

Introduction

I've collected recipes for more than fifty years. Many of these recipes were once written on cards and swapped with friends and family. I became interested in cooking when I worked at my mom and aunt's restaurant. The year I finished eighth grade, they took over a small restaurant in Allendale, Michigan, called the M-50 Drive In. It had three booths that seated four each, and a horseshoe-shaped bar with three stools on each side. So the whole place seated only twenty-one customers. We also did tray service to people who wanted to stay in their cars. Hamburgers were 25 cents and a hot beef sandwich with potatoes and gravy was 65 cents. My mom and Aunt Meme were great cooks, and I learned a lot from those two sisters. When Jim and I got married in 1964, I quickly learned that while I lived to eat, Jim ate to live. But he still very much enjoyed the meals I cooked. When the kids came home from school, they often asked, "What's for supper?" Those words are still music to my ears when the kids and grandkids come to my house. The delivery has changed; now the words often come in a text message. Technology has changed a lot. I still have those old recipe cards, but I also keep recipes on my iPad. One thing that hasn't changed is the joy of friends and family at the table for a wonderful meal. I hope you will be able to use the recipes in this book for your own fellowship and happiness.

—Joyce Klynstra

Favorites

So much of what you'll find in this book is kid-friendly. I asked my grandkids to tell me which recipes they like best. These are their picks.

MATTHEW'S PICK

Breakfast Pizza

PAGE 40

JOSEPH'S PICK

Caledonia Band Booster Chili

PAGE 60

LEVI'S PICK

Macaroni and Cheese

PAGE 127

MEGAN'S PICK

Karen's Strawberry Shortcake

PAGE 175

LEO'S PICK

Peanut Butter Balls

PAGE 218

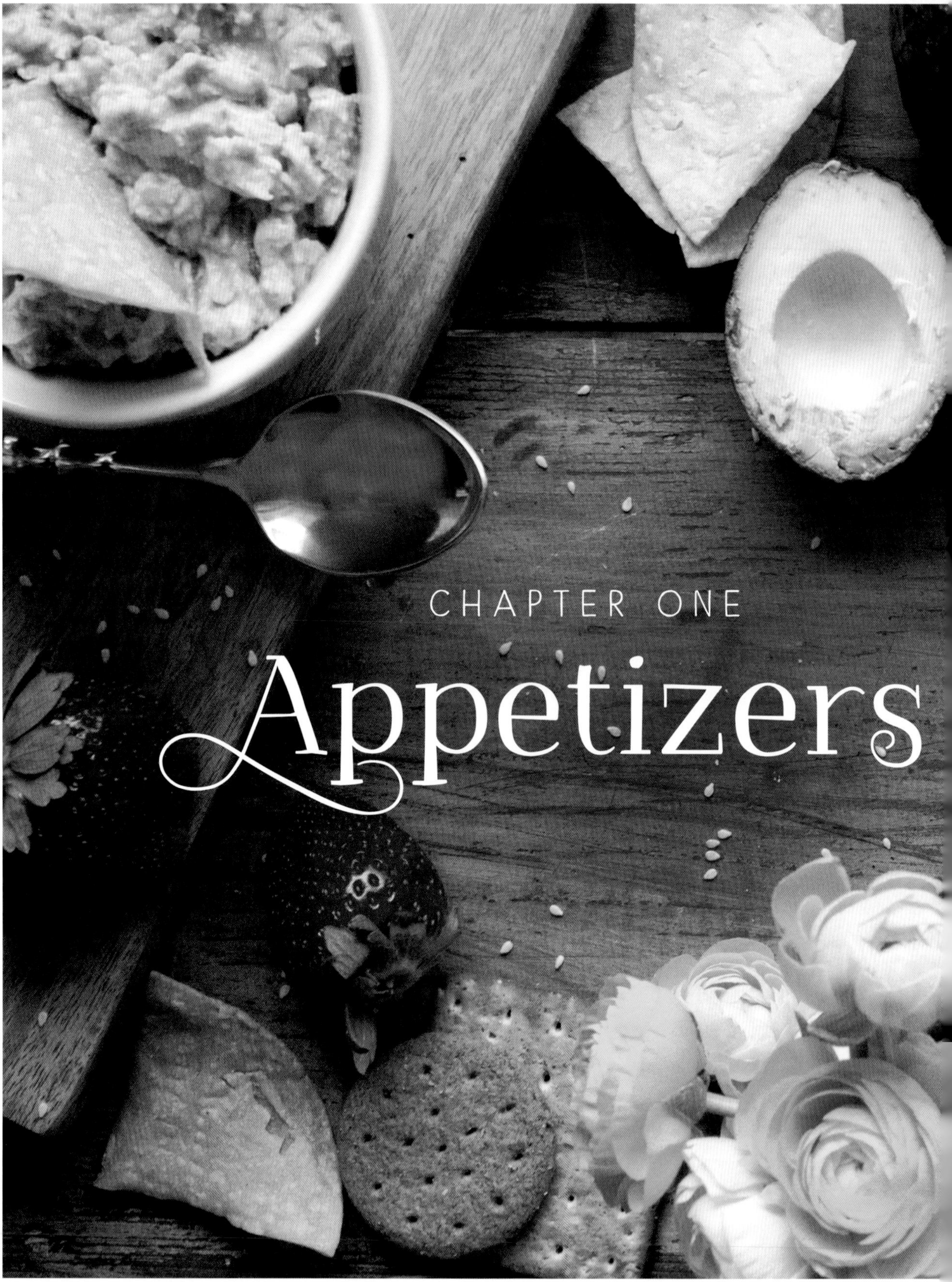

CHAPTER ONE

Appetizers

Asian Meatballs

These meatballs make a nice appetizer or you can serve them over rice for dinner.

SERVES **8–10**

2 pounds ground turkey
⅔ cup bread crumbs
5 scallions, chopped
2 eggs
2 tablespoons soy sauce
4 cloves garlic, chopped
2 teaspoons ginger
Salt and pepper to taste
1½ cups teriyaki sauce (recipe follows)

Preheat oven to 400°F.

In a large bowl, combine ground turkey, bread crumbs, scallions, eggs, soy sauce, garlic, ginger, and salt and pepper. Mix well and form into small balls.

Put on cookie sheet and bake about 15 minutes until meatballs are cooked through.

Place in slow cooker and pour teriyaki sauce over meatballs.

Heat in slow cooker on high for 20 minutes and serve. If you're serving these at a party, you can switch the slow cooker to low and keep them hot until you're ready to serve them.

Teriyaki Sauce

1 cup white sugar
1 cup brown sugar
1 cup soy sauce

Mix sauce ingredients and pour over whatever you desire. For the Asian Meatballs, half of this recipe works great.

Bleu Cheese Artichoke Appetizer

When my husband worked for the National Guard Association, I always made sure the hospitality room at conferences had lots of homemade snacks. This was a favorite served with chips or bread. Double the recipe if you have a big group.

2 ounces bleu cheese
2 sticks of butter
2 (14-ounce) can artichoke hearts, drained

SERVES **10**

Melt butter but don't boil. Crumble bleu cheese and stir into melted butter.

Cut artichokes in half and add to butter mixture.

Keep warm in slow cooker, fondue pot, or chafing dish.

Veggie Pizza

One of my daughter's friends used to request this appetizer when he visited. This one's for you, Howard! It's a delicious way to get your veggies.

2 tubes crescent rolls

16 ounces cream cheese

1 cup mayonnaise

1 (1-ounce) package ranch dressing seasoning mix

Chopped veggies, such as broccoli, cauliflower, green onions, shredded carrots, or any veggies you want to use.

2 cups shredded Colby cheese

Grape tomatoes, halved

SERVES **10**

Preheat oven to 375°F. Spread crescent rolls on cookie sheet. Bake for 15 to 20 minutes or until golden brown. Cool completely.

Mix cream cheese, mayonnaise, and ranch dressing mix until combined and spread on cooled crust. Cover with vegetables and cheese.

Cut in squares and put a grape tomato half on each piece.

Chili con Queso

This queso is always popular at a party. We ran out quickly at my grandson's graduation open house. Preparing the chilis is a little labor-intensive, but it's well worth the effort.

24 Anaheim chilis
4 medium Vidalia onions
3 medium tomatoes
1 pound Velveeta cheese, cubed
6 cups shredded Monterey Jack cheese
1½ cups half-and-half
5 cloves garlic, minced

SERVES **40**

Preheat broiler and line a large cookie sheet with foil. Cut chilis in half lengthwise; remove the stems and seeds. Place cut-side down on the prepared cookie sheet. Broil until the skins are blackened. If all the chilis don't fit on one pan, repeat this step with the remaining chilis.

Transfer charred chilis to a large paper bag, seal, and let steam for 10 minutes to soften skins.

Remove from bag. Peel and discard chili skins. Place the chilis, onions, and tomatoes in a large food processor and run until all the vegetables are finely chopped. If you don't have a large food processor, you can chop them manually. Set aside.

In a large saucepan, melt the cheeses over medium-low heat. When cheeses are melted, stir in cream and cook, stirring until smooth. Stir in chilies, onion, tomatoes, and garlic. Cook until the queso is hot all the way through.

Serve with chips or use to top off tacos or burrito bowls. You can store leftovers in the refrigerator for up to a week or divide into small sealed containers and freeze for up to 6 months.

Tip: If your grocery store is out of Anaheim chilis you can use 18 poblano chilis.

Joy's Olive Spread

If you like olives, you will love this spread. Put on crackers, sandwiches, or bagels.

MAKES 2½ CUPS

- 1 (5¾-ounce) jar chopped salad olives
- 1 (8-ounce) package cream cheese, softened
- ⅔ cup mayonnaise
- ¼ teaspoon black pepper
- ⅔ cup toasted chopped pecans

Drain and reserve liquid from olives.

Combine softened cream cheese, mayonnaise, and pepper. Mix well. Add 3 tablespoons of liquid from olives.

Fold in pecans and olives.

Taco in the Round

The friends that came to our hospitality room at National Guard Conferences always looked for this to be part of the party. Serve with corn chips.

SERVES **10**

- 1 pound ground beef
- 1 cup refried Beans (recipe page 124)
- 2 Tablespoons homemade taco seasoning (recipe below)
- 1 cup salsa
- 1 (8-ounce) package cream cheese, softened
- ½ cup cottage cheese
- 2 tablespoons sour cream
- 1½ teaspoons chili powder
- Salt and pepper to taste
- 8 ounce grated cheddar cheese
- Lettuce
- Tomato

Brown ground beef, drain. Add refried beans and taco seasoning to beef. Spread on serving plate and cool.

Spread salsa on ground beef.

Mix cream cheese, cottage cheese, sour cream, chili powder and salt and pepper with a mixer and spread over salsa.

Top with lettuce, cheese and tomato. Serve with corn chips.

Homemade Taco Seasoning

- 2 tablespoons chili powder
- ½ teaspoon garlic powder
- ½ teaspoon onion powder
- ¼ teaspoon ground red pepper
- ½ teaspoon oregano
- 1 teaspoon paprika
- 1 tablespoon cumin
- 2½ teaspoons salt
- 1 teaspoons pepper

Combine all ingredients. Mix well and store in tightly closed container. Use 2 tablespoons per pound of ground beef or to taste.

Guacamole Dip

I came across this dip in Hawaii's hospitality room at a National Guard Conference, and they were nice enough to share the recipe with me. It's a fast and easy dip. Serve with tortilla chips or with your favorite Mexican meal.

3 avocados
1 tablespoon lemon juice
½ teaspoon salt
½ cup your favorite salsa
¼ cup sour cream

SERVES **6**

Cut avocados in half. Remove pit. Scoop avacado out of the skin and place in a medium bowl. Mash avocados. Stir in lemon juice and salt. Then add salsa and sour cream.

Serve immediately.

CHAPTER TWO

Breads

Six-Week Bran Muffins

Baked goods are best fresh out of the oven. This dough will keep six weeks in an airtight container in the refrigerator. You can make a few hot muffins in minutes and reserve the dough for the next time you want a hot bran muffin.

- 14 tablespoons (¾ cup + 2 tablespoons) shortening
- 1¾ cups boiling water
- 3 cups sugar
- 2½ teaspoons salt
- 4 beaten eggs
- 6¼ cups flour
- 7¼ cups (18.3-ounce box) All-Bran Original
- 3½ cups buttermilk
- 2 tablespoons baking soda

MAKES **5** TO **6** DOZEN

These muffins are best mixed by hand.

Melt the shortening in boiling water; set aside to cool.

In large bowl, mix sugar, salt, eggs, and cooled shortening-and-water mixture. Mix well.

Add flour and All-Bran to the shortening mixture. Mix well.

Dissolve baking soda in buttermilk. Fold into the batter.

Store batter in refrigerator for up to six weeks and bake each serving fresh.

To bake: Fill greased muffin pan almost level full. Bake at 350°F for 20 minutes or until firm to the touch.

Banana Bread

This banana bread is so moist and delicious. It's a really great way to use up those bananas that got too ripe. If you have a lot of bananas, make more loaves of bread and store them in the freezer.

MAKES **1** LOAF

- 1 cup sugar
- ½ cup butter
- 2 eggs
- 1 cup bananas, mashed
- ½ cup sour cream
- 1 teaspoon vanilla extract
- 1½ cups flour
- ½ teaspoon salt
- 1 teaspoon baking soda

Preheat oven to 350°F. Grease a 9 x 5-inch loaf pan and set aside.

In a medium bowl, cream sugar and butter. Mix in eggs, bananas, sour cream, and vanilla.

In a separate bowl, whisk together flour, salt, and baking soda. Add to butter mixture.

Pour into prepared pan. Bake for 50 minutes or until toothpick comes out clean. Cool 10 minutes and then turn out onto cutting board. Slice and serve warm.

Beer Bread

This bread is amazing and deceptively simple. It pairs well with soup or as a side with dinner. The beer you choose will change the flavor.

MAKES **1** LOAF

- 3 tablespoons salted butter
- 1 tablespoon olive oil
- 3 cups flour, plus more for pan
- 3 tablespoons sugar
- 1 tablespoon baking powder
- 1 teaspoon salt
- 1 (12-ounce) can or bottle of beer at room temperature

Preheat oven to 350°F. Grease and flour a 9 x 5-inch loaf pan and set aside.

Melt butter and mix in olive oil. Set aside.

Whisk together flour, sugar, baking powder, salt. Add beer and stir just until combined. Batter should be slightly lumpy; don't overmix.

Put in prepared pan and drizzle with butter mixture.

Bake 35 to 40 minutes or until toothpick comes out clean. Turn out onto a cutting board, slice, and serve warm.

Easy Biscuits

I love this recipe because there is no butter to cut into the flour. You just mix in the whipping cream. (They are delicious, too!)

MAKES **9**

- 2 cups self-rising flour
- 2 tablespoons sugar
- 1⅓ cups whipping cream

Preheat oven to 450°F.

Mix flour and sugar and add whipping cream. Mix until dough forms and put dough on floured surface.

Flatten dough, fold in half, and repeat two more times. Pat dough into a 6-inch square about ¾ inch thick.

Cut into 9 squares and put on greased cookie sheet. Brush tops with more cream.

Bake about 12 minutes until golden brown.

Blueberry Muffins

Serve these wonderful muffins warm with butter. They make a nice addition to your breakfast or brunch menus or taste great with a cup of coffee anytime.

- 1 cup sugar + more for tops
- 2 tablespoons melted butter
- 1 egg
- 1 cup sour cream
- 1¾ cups flour
- 1 teaspoon baking soda
- 1 teaspoon baking powder
- 1 teaspoon salt
- 1½ cups blueberries

MAKES **12** MUFFINS

Preheat oven to 350°F.

Blend first four ingredients. Mix flour, baking soda, baking powder, and salt and add to first mixture.

Mix lightly and fold in blueberries.

Pour in greased and floured 12-muffin pan.

Sprinkle tops with sugar.

Bake for 20 minutes.

Bread Machine Honey Oatmeal Bread

I love to bring my bread machine along on family vacations. Every time I bake a loaf it disappears in no time.

MAKES **1** LARGE LOAF

1¼ cups warm water
½ cup honey
2 tablespoons vegetable oil
1 cup quick oats
1½ teaspoons salt
3 cups + 2 tablespoons bread flour
2¼ teaspoons active dry yeast

Into bread machine pan, pour ingredients in order listed.

Select basic bread setting.

After it mixes a few minutes, check to see if it might need a tablespoon of water (if the dough looks too dry).

When bread finishes baking, turn out onto a cutting board, slice, and serve warm.

Zucchini Bread

In the late summer, when zucchinis are plentiful, bake up a couple batches of this moist bread. Freeze the loaves you don't use right away or share them with friends.

MAKES **2** LOAVES

- 3 cups flour, plus more for pans
- 1 teaspoon salt
- 1 teaspoon baking soda
- 1 teaspoon baking powder
- 1 tablespoon cinnamon
- 3 eggs
- 1 cup vegetable oil
- 2 cups sugar
- 1 tablespoon vanilla extract
- 2 cups grated zucchini
- 1 cup chopped walnuts or pecans (optional)

Preheat oven to 325°F. Grease and flour two 9 x 5-inch loaf pans.

Whisk together flour, salt, baking powder, baking soda, and cinnamon.

In a large bowl, beat eggs, oil, vanilla, and sugar together with a hand mixer. Add dry ingredients and mix well.

Fold in zucchini and nuts.

Put in prepared pans and bake 45 to 55 minutes or until tester comes out clean.

Cool in pans for 15 minutes and then turn out onto a cutting board, slice, and serve warm.

CHAPTER THREE

Breakfast

Crustless Avocado Quiche

I make this when I want to have a gluten-free option for guests. It's so good you will never miss the crust.

SERVES **8**

- 9 eggs
- ⅓ cup milk
- ½ teaspoon salt
- ¼ teaspoon pepper
- ⅔ cup shredded mozzarella cheese
- 1 pound sausage, browned and drained
- 2 avocados, peeled, seeded, and diced

Preheat oven to 350°F. Coat a pie plate with nonstick spray.

Beat eggs, milk, salt, and pepper. Add cheese, sausage, and avocado. Mix well and pour into prepared pie plate.

Bake 30 to 45 minutes or until a knife comes out clean when inserted.

You can substitute crisp bacon pieces or ham for the sausage.

Baked French Toast

I like having this make-ahead French toast in the refrigerator in the morning, ready to bake. Serve with warm pure maple syrup, berries, and whipped cream.

SERVES **8**

½ cup butter
1 cup packed brown sugar
2 teaspoons vanilla extract, divided
1 loaf French bread cut in 1-inch slices
1½ cups milk
6 eggs
2 tablespoons pure maple syrup
½ teaspoon salt
1 teaspoon cinnamon

Coat a jelly-roll pan with nonstick spray.

In a small saucepan, melt butter and brown sugar; stir until smooth. Add 1 teaspoon of vanilla extract. Pour mixture onto prepared jelly-roll pan.

Arrange sliced bread in single layer to cover pan.

Beat eggs and whisk in milk, maple syrup, remaining teaspoon of vanilla, salt, and cinnamon. Spoon this mixture over bread. Cover and refrigerate overnight.

When ready to bake, preheat oven to 350°F.

Bake uncovered for 25 to 30 minutes.

Serve immediately.

Breakfast Pizza

This is a favorite breakfast on family vacations and holiday mornings. If you like breakfast for dinner, this is a great go-to recipe.

2 tubes of crescent rolls
1 pound sausage, browned
2½ cups hash brown potatoes
8 ounces shredded Colby jack cheese
¼ cup Parmesan cheese
1 dozen eggs
1 tablespoon Worcestershire sauce
1 teaspoon dry mustard
1 teaspoon salt
1¾ cups milk

SERVES **10**

Preheat oven to 350°F.

Line jelly-roll pan with crescent rolls. Push the dough up the sides and seal the seams.

Layer sausage, hash browns, and cheeses on dough.

In a medium bowl, beat eggs, Worcestershire sauce, dry mustard, salt, and milk with a whisk. Pour over sausage, hash browns, and cheese.

Bake for 45 minutes or until the middle is firmly set.

MATTHEW'S PICK

Buttermilk Pancakes with Blueberry Sauce

It really doesn't take much time to make pancakes from scratch and it's so worth it. Using buttermilk makes them so much better.

MAKES **10** MEDIUM PANCAKES

- 2 cups flour
- 3 tablespoons brown sugar
- 1½ teaspoons baking powder
- 1 teaspoon baking soda
- 1 teaspoon salt
- 2 cups buttermilk
- 2 eggs
- 3 tablespoons vegetable oil
- Fresh blueberries (optional)
- Salted butter for the griddle

Preheat cast-iron griddle over medium heat.

Combine flour, sugar, baking powder, baking soda, and salt.

Whisk together buttermilk, eggs, and oil.

Add buttermilk mixture into flour mixture. Do not overmix. Batter will be slightly lumpy.

Generously butter the preheated griddle. Pour about ¼ cup batter onto the griddle. If using, add blueberries to the batter as it cooks. Cook about 3 to 4 minutes until tops are bubbly. Flip to cook the other side.

Repeat until batter is gone. Reapply butter to the griddle between pancakes.

Serve hot with pure maple syrup or blueberry sauce.

Blueberry Sauce

MAKES 1⅓ CUPS

- 1 tablespoon butter
- 1 pint blueberries
- ¼ cup pure maple syrup

Melt butter in saucepan, add blueberries and maple syrup, and cook until blueberries release juice. Cool a little and serve over ice cream, pancakes, or waffles.

Pig in Blankets

I like to keep some of these in the freezer for a quick and easy breakfast or for unexpected guests any time of the day.

MEAT MIXTURE

1 pound ground beef
1 pound bulk sausage
2 eggs
¾ cup oatmeal
1 teaspoon salt

DOUGH

3 cups flour + extra
2 sticks butter
1 tablespoon baking powder
1 teaspoon salt
3 tablespoons sugar
1 cup milk

MAKES **32**

Combine meat mixture and form into 32 pigs. Place in refrigerator.

Mix dough ingredients with a pastry blender. Divide the dough into four equal parts. Roll out the first quarter of dough on a floured surface. Cut out 3¾-inch circles, using a cookie cutter or the top of a glass.

Remove pigs from the refrigerator. Wrap dough around meat and place seam side down on cookie sheet.

Repeat with remaining dough and pigs.

Bake at 400°F for 30 minutes. Or freeze to use later.

To freeze: Place on a parchment-lined cookie sheet. Make sure none of the pigs are touching. Place the cookie sheet in the freezer for 4 hours. After the pigs are frozen, take off cookie sheet and store in freezer bags in freezer for up to three months.

Sausage Egg and Cheese Breakfast Braid

When you have overnight guests, impress them with this beautiful breakfast braid. It pairs well with muffins and fresh fruit.

½ cup milk
4 ounces softened cream cheese
10 eggs
½ teaspoon garlic powder
½ teaspoon onion powder
Salt and pepper to taste
2 teaspoons butter
2 packages crescent rolls
1 pound sausage, browned and drained, 1 package of bacon, cooked, drained, and crumbled, or thinly sliced ham
1¼ cups shredded cheese

SERVES **8**

Preheat oven to 375°F. Coat a large cookie sheet with cooking spray and set aside.

With an electric hand mixer, mix milk and cream cheese. Beat in eggs and seasonings.

In a larger frying pan over medium heat, melt butter. Cook egg mixture until almost done. Eggs should still be a little runny.

Unroll one package of crescent rolls, without separating, on the prepared cookie sheet. This will form the rectangle-shaped base of your braid. Separate second package of crescent rolls into the pre-cut triangles. Attach the edge of each triangle to the edge of the base dough with triangle points pointing out.

Spoon sausage, bacon, or ham on rectangle. Top the meat with the egg mixture and cheese.

Bring corners of crescent rolls over cheese to form a braid.

Bake for 25 minutes until the dough is golden brown.

CHAPTER FOUR

Soups

Dutch Pea Soup

Pea soup is a traditional part of my Dutch heritage. I remember eating this since childhood, and it's still one of my favorites.

SERVES **8**

1 pound split peas
5 cups water
32 ounces vegetable broth
1 bay leaf
1 meaty ham bone
2 potatoes, diced
3 carrots, sliced
1 large onion, diced
Salt and pepper to taste

Put peas, water, vegetable broth, bay leaf, and ham bone in large pot and simmer for 1½ hours.

Take ham bone out and set aside to cool. Remove bay leaf and discard.

Add vegetables to pot and simmer for 30 minutes or until vegetables are tender.

When ham bone has cooled enough to handle, cut meat from the bone. Place meat in the soup and heat through.

Add salt and pepper to taste.

Creamy Slow Cooker Potato Soup

If you want to come home to soup in your slow cooker, try this easy potato soup.

SERVES **6**

32 ounces frozen hash brown potatoes
32 ounces chicken broth
1 (8-ounce) package cream cheese, cut in small pieces
¼ cup butter, cut in small pieces
1 cup shredded Colby jack cheese
Salt and pepper to taste
Chives (optional)
Crumbled bacon (optional)

Place all ingredients in slow cooker and stir. Cook 3 hours on high or 6 hours on low.

Mix thoroughly. Garnish with chives, crumbled bacon, and black pepper if using.

Dutch Pea Soup
PAGE 50

Chicken Soup
PAGE 54
Creamy Slow Cooker Potato Soup
PAGE 51

Chicken Soup

My chicken soup makes a great meal with plenty of rice and vegetables. A cinnamon stick rounds out the flavor and makes this soup unique.

8 cups chicken broth
1 pound skinless chicken breast
1 cinnamon stick
4 carrots, peeled and sliced
1 onion, chopped
4 stalks celery, sliced
½ cup uncooked white rice
Salt and pepper to taste

SERVES 4

Place the chicken broth, chicken, and cinnamon stick in a large pot and boil until chicken is cooked all the way through. Take chicken out of pan and place on a cutting board to cool.

Add carrots, onion, and celery in saucepan with the broth. Bring to boil then reduce heat and cook covered until vegetables are almost tender.

When the chicken is cool enough to handle, cut into small pieces and return it to the pot.

Add rice and simmer for about 15 minutes or until rice is done.

Remove cinnamon stick and discard.

Add salt and pepper to taste.

Broccoli Soup

This is creamy, cheesy comfort in a bowl. Just bake some potatoes and make a loaf of beer bread (page 25) and it's a nice cool-weather meal.

SERVES **6**

- 12 tablespoons butter, divided
- 1½ cups chopped carrots
- 1 onion
- 2 stalks celery
- 2 (14½-ounce) cans chicken broth
- 4 cups broccoli heads
- ½ cup flour
- 2 cups milk
- ½ cup shredded Colby cheese
- 1 (8-ounce) jar Cheez Whiz
- Salt and pepper to taste

Using a food processor, finely chop carrots, onion, and celery.

In a large skillet, sauté the vegetables in 6 tablespoons of the butter. When vegetables are almost tender, add chicken broth and broccoli heads.

Cook until broccoli is tender. Set aside.

In another pan, melt remaining butter; add flour, and whisk into a paste. Gradually add 2 cups milk; whisk and cook until thick.

Add shredded cheese and Cheez Whiz. When cheese is melted, add to vegetable mixture and heat until hot.

Add salt and pepper to taste

Vegetable Beef Soup

The largest section in my recipe box is definitely soups; of my many recipes, this has been one of my favorites for years.

SERVES **6**

- 1 meaty beef soup bone
- 6 cups water
- 2 beef bouillon cubes
- 2 (14½-ounce) cans beef broth
- 2 large carrots, sliced
- 2 stalks celery, sliced
- 1 onion, chopped fine
- ⅓–½ cup uncooked rice, depending how thick you like it
- 2 (14½-ounce) cans diced tomatoes
- Salt and pepper to taste

In a large pot, simmer bone, water, bouillon cubes, and beef broth, covered, until meat is very tender. This will take 1 hour or longer.

Take meat out and set aside to cool.

Add vegetables and rice to the liquid in the pan, and simmer until vegetables are almost tender.

Add tomatoes and salt and pepper.

When the meat bone is cool enough to handle, cut off meat into small pieces. Add meat to the pot.

Cook until vegetables and rice are soft.

If it's too thick, you can add more beef broth or water.

Vegetable Beef Soup
PAGE 56
Broccoli Soup
PAGE 55

Butternut Squash Soup

This soup brings out all the delicious flavors of autumn. If you're like me and don't enjoy peeling squash, buy cleaned and diced squash. It saves a lot of time—and your fingers, too.

SERVES **8**

- 1 large butternut squash or 2 pounds cleaned and cut squash
- 1 large onion, diced
- 3 tablespoons olive oil
- Salt and pepper to taste
- 1½ cups apple juice
- 1 (14½-ounce) can of pumpkin
- 1½ cups vegetable or chicken broth
- 1½ cups half-and-half
- 2 tablespoons honey
- ½ teaspoon cinnamon
- 1 tablespoon sugar
- ¼ teaspoon curry powder
- 1 teaspoon salt
- ¼ teaspoon pepper

Preheat oven to 400°F.

Peel and seed squash and cut into chunks or use the squash that is already prepared.

Place squash and diced onion on a cookie sheet. Drizzle with oil and sprinkle with salt and pepper. Bake for about 30 minutes or until fork tender.

Purée squash with apple juice in a blender.

Pour into a large pot. Add pumpkin, half-and-half, broth, honey, seasonings, and sugar.

Simmer for 15 minutes.

If it's too thick, you can thin with more broth or half-and-half.

Caledonia Band Booster Chili

This recipe is based on my favorite chili from my grandson's band booster chili cook-off. The mom who made it was kind and shared the recipe with me. I tweaked it a bit to my tastes, and made it a little more diet friendly.

SERVES **12**

1 pound 90% lean ground beef
1 pound lean ground turkey
1 teaspoon salt
¾ cup diced onion
1 (48-ounce) jar of Randall mixed beans
1 (14½ ounce) can beef broth
1 package mild chili mix
1 (10-ounce) can mild Ro*Tel tomatoes
1 pint stewed tomatoes (page 227)
2 tablespoons molasses
¼ cup barbecue sauce
1 tablespoon brown sugar

Brown ground beef, ground turkey, salt, and onions in a frying pan. Drain grease and discard.

Move the ground beef, ground turkey, and onions to a large pot. Add the remaining ingredients. Simmer on medium-low heat for 30 minutes.

Dutch Meatball Soup

I love to swap recipes with my friends. I first tried this at a youth soup luncheon at my church. I highly recommend serving with beer bread (page 25).

SERVES **6**

MEATBALLS

1 pound ground beef
1 teaspoon salt
½ teaspoon nutmeg
½ teaspoon pepper
2 eggs
15 crackers, crushed

SOUP

4 quarts chicken broth
2 leeks, chopped
⅔ cup celery
2 carrots, chopped
⅓ cup white rice
2 cups uncooked noodles
1 teaspoon parsley

Preheat over to 350°F.

Mix the meatball ingredients and form into small meatballs.

Place on cookie sheet and bake at 350°F until done, about 15 minutes.

In a large pot over medium-high heat, bring broth to boil and add leeks, celery, and carrots.

Simmer for about 20 minutes or until vegetables are tender.

Add meatballs and rice. Simmer 10 minutes.

Add noodles and parsley, and cook 15 minutes until noodles are done.

Polish Kielbasa Slow Cooker Soup

Add a salad and garlic bread to the table along with this soup and you have dinner.

SERVES **8**

1½ pounds Polish kielbasa
1 tablespoon olive oil
6 potatoes, chopped
1 onion, chopped
1 tablespoon minced garlic
32 ounces chicken broth
1 cup half-and-half
2 tablespoons flour
1½ cups chopped kale
Salt and pepper to taste

Cut kielbasa in half lengthwise and then slice. Brown kielbasa in frying pan in olive oil.

Place kielbasa, potatoes, onion, garlic, and chicken broth in a slow cooker. If needed, add water to just cover vegetables and kielbasa.

Cook on high for 3 to 4 hours, or 5 to 6 hours on low, until potatoes are soft.

About an hour before serving, whisk flour into half-and-half.

Add cream mixture and kale to slow cooker and stir.

Cook on high until broth thickens slightly, about 1 hour.

Add salt and pepper to taste.

Beef, Beer, and Barley Soup

I make this soup when I have leftover beef roast. Serve with warm biscuits or fresh dinner rolls and a salad.

32 ounces beef broth
1½ cups sliced carrots
1 cup diced onion
1 cup chopped celery
1 teaspoon garlic powder
1 teaspoon onion powder
2½ cups leftover beef roast
½ cup quick-cooking barley
¾ cup dark beer
Salt and pepper to taste

SERVES **6–8**

Add broth, vegetables, and seasonings to a large pot and cook over medium-high heat. Cook until vegetables are tender, about 20 minutes.

Add beef, barley, and beer and simmer covered for 30 minutes. Add salt and pepper to taste.

Beef, Beer, and Barley Soup
PAGE 65
Vegetable Cheese Soup
PAGE 67
Polish Kielbasa Slow Cooker Soup
PAGE 64

Vegetable Cheese Soup

This is a quick and easy pot of soup. You can make it vegetarian by leaving out the ham.

SERVES **8–10**

1 large onion, diced
1 cup water
2 cups chopped ham (optional)
1 (12-ounce) bag frozen broccoli
1 (12-ounce) bag frozen cauliflower
4 cans (10½-ounce) Campbell's Cheddar Cheese Soup
1 quart half-and-half

Simmer onions, ham (if using), broccoli, and cauliflower in the water until vegetables are tender, about 20 minutes.

Add soup and half-and-half.

Heat through.

Potato Cheese Soup

I love a potato soup at a popular local restaurant. So I came up with this recipe, and I think I came very close.

3 cups vegetable or chicken broth
4 medium potatoes, peeled and diced
1 carrot, sliced
1 stalk celery, cut in small slices
1 medium onion, chopped
1 cup half-and-half
1 cup shredded cheddar cheese
¼ cup butter
Salt and pepper to taste

SERVES **6**

Add broth, vegetables, and seasonings to a large pot and cook over medium-high heat. Cook until vegetables are tender, about 25 to 30 minutes.

Pour in blender and purée.

Return puréed vegetables to pot. Add half-and-half, cheese, and butter. Stir and heat through until cheese is melted and combined.

Add salt and pepper to taste.

CHAPTER FIVE

Main Dishes

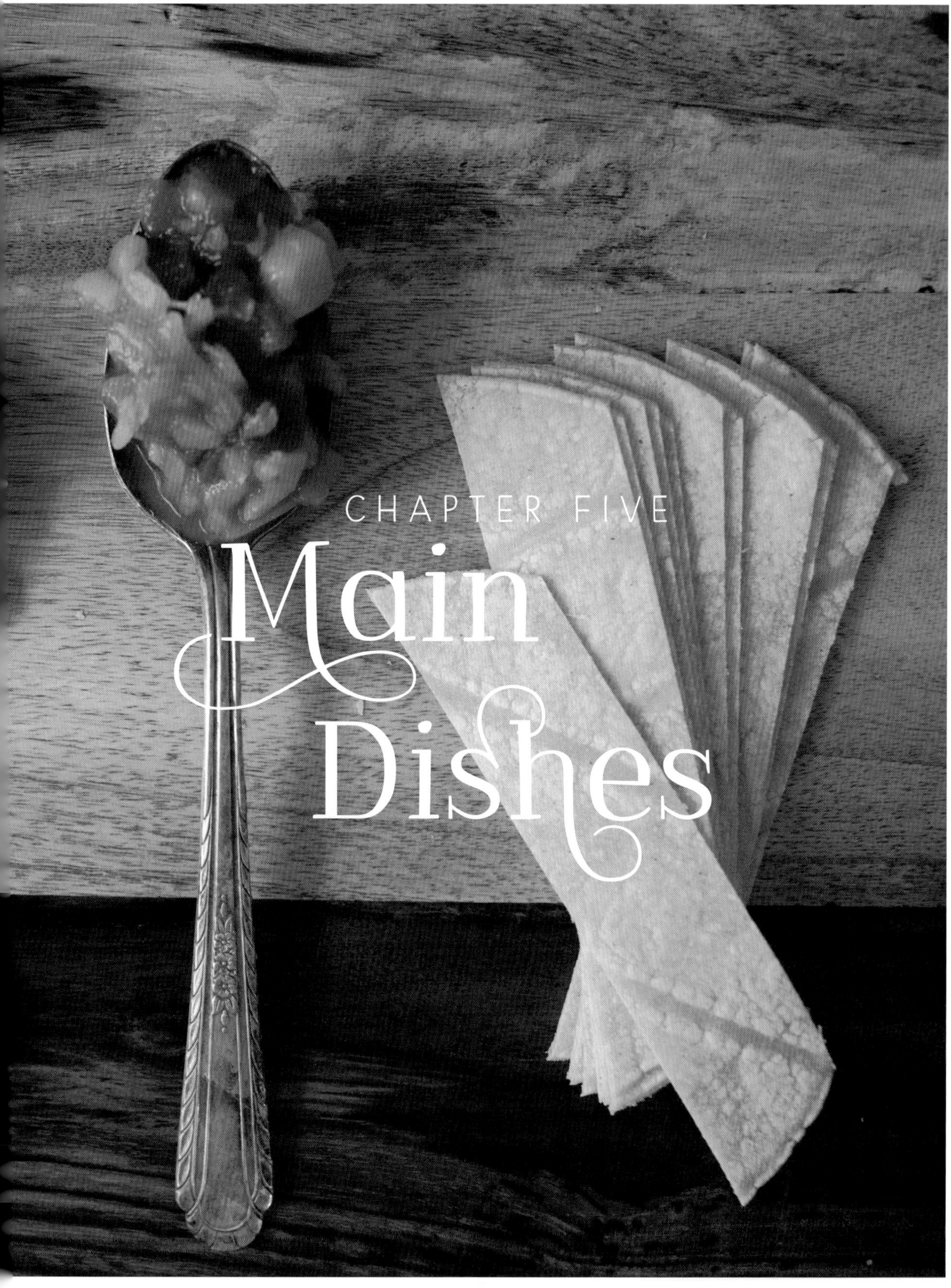

Wet Burritos

This Tex-Mex-inspired dish is popular in Michigan. It has all the deliciousness of a burrito, with the sauce-and-cheese goodness of an enchilada.

SERVES 4

- 1 pound ground beef
- Homemade taco seasoning (see page 14)
- 4 extra-large flour tortillas
- 1½ cups refried beans (see page 124)
- 1 quart burrito sauce (see page 225)
- 8 ounces shredded Colby jack cheese
- 1 bunch scallions, chopped finely
- 1 head romaine, chopped finely
- Sour cream (optional)

Preheat oven to 350°F.

Brown ground beef in a medium frying pan. Drain and add seasoning.

Warm refried beans.

Fill each tortilla with ground beef and beans. Roll tortilla and fold the ends. Place in a casserole dish.

Cover the burritos with sauce and then cheese. Bake for 15 minutes or just until the cheese is melted.

Cover each serving in romaine and scallions to taste. Serve with sour cream, if using.

You can make individual burritos by providing a spread of ingredients. Let each person build his/her own burrito, cover in sauce and cheese, and microwave until cheese is melted.

American Goulash

A classic Midwestern comfort food, this recipe is nothing like Hungarian goulash. My son loved it when he was growing up.

SERVES **6**

- 1 pound ground beef
- 1 medium onion, diced
- 1 pint stewed tomatoes (see page 227)
- 1 (10½-ounce) can tomato soup
- 1 pound elbow pasta cooked according to package directions, drained
- ¼ cup butter

In a large frying pan, cook ground beef and onion until beef is brown and onion is tender. Drain.

Add stewed tomatoes, tomato soup, and prepared pasta.

Let simmer 5 minutes, stirring often to prevent sticking to the pan.

Add butter, and when melted and combined, serve.

Swiss Cheese Chicken and Mushroom Bake

Bring the flavors of Thanksgiving to any day with this easy chicken dish. Pair it with mashed potatoes and a vegetable for a great meal.

- 6 boneless, skinless chicken breast halves
- 1 cup shredded Swiss cheese
- ½ pound fresh mushrooms
- 1 (10½-ounce) can cream of mushroom soup
- 1 (10½-ounce) can cream of chicken soup
- 1 cup Pepperidge Farm Herb Seasoned Stuffing mix

SERVES **6**

Preheat oven to 350°F.

Clean chicken and place in a 9 x 13-inch pan.

Cover chicken with cheese and mushrooms.

Mix soups together and spread over chicken.

Sprinkle stuffing on top.

Bake uncovered for 40 to 50 minutes or until chicken is done.

Chicken Pot Pie

I like to use store-bought pie crust for this pot pie. If you have leftover chicken to use, you have a quick meal on your hands!

SERVES **6–8**

- 2 unbaked pie crusts
- 1 (29-ounce) can of Veg-All homestyle large cut vegetables
- 2 (10½-ounce) cans cream of potato soup
- 2 cups cooked diced chicken
- ¼ teaspoon thyme
- ½ cup milk
- 1 beaten egg

Preheat oven to 375°F.

Put one crust in 9-inch pie plate.

Mix Veg-All, soup, chicken, thyme, and milk in a medium bowl.

Put vegetable mixture in crust.

Cover with the second crust. Crimp and seal edges.

Slit top crust and brush with beaten egg.

Bake for 40 minutes.

Leah's Chicken Squares

My cousin and good friend shared this recipe with me many years ago. It's a great dish for showers or parties.

- 1½ pounds chicken breast
- 1 (8-ounce) package cream cheese
- 8 tablespoons butter, divided
- ¼ teaspoon poultry seasoning
- Salt and pepper to taste
- 4 tablespoons milk
- 2 tablespoons finely diced onion
- 2 packages crescent rolls
- 1½ cups Pepperidge Farm Herb Seasoned Stuffing mix

MAKES **8**

Preheat oven to 375°F.

Boil chicken breasts until cooked through. Drain. When chicken is cool enough to handle, cut it into small pieces. Set aside.

Combine cream cheese and 4 tablespoons butter in a heat-proof bowl and soften in microwave.

Add salt, pepper, poultry seasoning, milk, and onion to the cream cheese mixture. Stir in chicken.

Divide crescent rolls into 8 rectangles and put ½ cup mixture on each rectangle.

Fold rolls over chicken mixture and pinch ends closed.

Melt 4 tablespoons butter and dip tops in butter and then in stuffing mix or crushed croutons.

Bake for 20 minutes or until golden brown.

Chicken Tater Tot Casserole

This casserole has been a favorite of our family for years. You can replace the fresh corn with frozen corn to make it even easier.

SERVES **6–8**

- 4 chicken breast
- 4 ears of corn
- 1 (10½-ounce) can cream of mushroom soup
- 1 (10½-ounce) can cream of chicken soup
- 1 stack Ritz crackers, crushed
- 8 ounces grated mild cheddar cheese
- 1 (32-ounce) package frozen tater tots

Preheat oven to at 350°F.

In a medium pot, boil chicken until cooked through. Set aside chicken to cool and reserve 1 cup of broth.

In a separate pot, boil corn cobs for 10 minutes. Remove from water to cool.

Mix soups and reserved broth and set aside.

When chicken is cool enough to handle, cut into small pieces and set aside.

With a sharp knife, cut the corn off the cob directly into a 9 x 13-inch pan. Cover the bottom of the pan with the corn. Layer diced chicken, cracker crumbs, and cheese on top of the corn.

Pour the soup mixture over other ingredients and top with tater tots.

Bake for 45 minutes. The edges of the casserole should be bubbling, and the tater tots should be golden brown.

Tortilla Chicken Casserole

The green chilies give this casserole a ton of flavor. It pairs nicely with corn cake (see page 120).

SERVES **8**

- 3 chicken breasts
- 2 (10½-ounce) cans of cream mushroom soup
- 1 (10½-ounce) can of cream chicken soup
- 1 cup sour cream
- 1 small can sliced olives, drained
- 1 small can green chilies, drained
- 1 small onion, diced
- 8 corn tortillas, cut in strips
- 8 ounces shredded cheddar cheese

Preheat oven to at 350°F.

Rinse chicken breasts and place in a medium pot; fill with enough water to cover chicken. Boil chicken until cooked through. You can check for doneness by cutting with kitchen shears. Set aside chicken to cool and reserve broth.

When chicken is cool enough to handle, cut into small pieces and set aside.

Mix together soups, ¾ cup of reserved broth, sour cream, olives, chilies, and onion.

Layer ingredients in 9 x 13-inch casserole dish: start with half of sauce mixture, then half of the tortilla strips, chicken, and cheese. Repeat layers, ending with cheese.

Bake covered for 1 hour.

Corn Dogs

Corn dogs remind me of summers spent at Lake Michigan. These tend to come out a bit messy, but they taste amazing.

MAKES **8**

- ½ cup cornmeal
- 1½ cups flour
- 4 teaspoons baking powder
- 2 teaspoons salt
- ¼ cup sugar
- 1 egg
- 1 cup milk
- 3 cups vegetable oil for frying
- 8 hot dogs
- Wooden sticks

In a medium bowl, whisk together dry ingredients. Add egg and milk. Set aside.

Preheat oil in a deep frying pan or pot. Make sure the pan is wide enough to accommodate the hot dog and stick. The oil should be 2 inches deep. For best results, use a candy thermometer to monitor the temperature of the oil. When the oil reaches 350°F, it is ready.

Pierce each hot dog at one end with a stick. Dip the hot dog in the batter until it's coated.

Fry in preheated oil until golden brown. Remove from the oil with tongs and transfer to paper towels to drain any excess oil. Top with your favorite hot dog condiments and serve immediately.

Creamed Chicken on Biscuits
PAGE 90
Creamed Asparagus on Biscuits
PAGE 89

Creamed Asparagus on Biscuits

My mom made this recipe when asparagus was in season. She didn't use measuring cups, but I've worked out the amounts. My mom served it on toast but it's even better on fresh biscuits.

2 pounds asparagus
1½ cups milk
3 tablespoons butter
¾ cup water
⅓ cup flour
Salt
Pepper
4 biscuits (page 26)

SERVES 4 AS A MEAL

Trim asparagus and discard the hard part of the stem. Cut asparagus in small pieces and boil in salted water until tender but still somewhat crisp. Drain.

Add milk and butter to asparagus and bring to boil.

Put water and flour in a container with a tight cover and shake to dissolve flour.

Add to boiling milk/asparagus mixture. Bring back to boil for about 5 minutes or until the mixture thickens.

Add salt and pepper to taste.

Serve over biscuits.

Creamed Chicken on Biscuits

I used to cook this for our family-night dinners at church. It's easy to make a large batch for a group. It was one of their favorites. You can also try this if you have leftover turkey after Thanksgiving.

SERVES **8**

6 tablespoons butter
1½ cups diced celery
½ cup diced onion
1 cup frozen peas (optional)
6 tablespoons flour
¾ cup milk
3 cups chicken broth
Salt and pepper to taste
4½ cups diced cooked chicken or turkey
8 biscuits (page 26)

In a deep frying pan, over medium heat, cook celery and onion in butter until tender, then add peas if using.

Stir in flour. Add milk and stir until well blended.

Add broth slowly. Stir in salt and pepper to taste.

Cook until it thickens. You may have to mix with a wire whisk to prevent lumps.

Add chicken or turkey and cook until heated through.

Serve over biscuits.

Swedish Meatballs

You can serve these meatballs as a nice appetizer or a great dinner over rice or noodles. Serve with a salad or your favorite vegetable if using for dinner.

SERVES **6** AS A MEAL

MEATBALLS

1 pound ground beef
1 egg
⅓ cup oatmeal
⅓ cup milk

SAUCE

1 (10½-ounce) can cream of mushroom soup
¾ cup milk
4 ounces softened cream cheese
2 tablespoons ketchup
⅛ teaspoon garlic powder
1 cup sour cream
8 ounces noodles, cooked and drained (optional)

Preheat oven to 350°F.

Mix meatball ingredients. Form into balls and place on cookie sheet.

Bake on a cookie sheet for 15 to 20 minutes.

In a medium pot, combine soup, milk, cream cheese, ketchup, and garlic powder.

Cook and stir over low heat until blended.

Stir in meatballs and cover and simmer 10 minutes.

Stir in sour cream. Heat through, but do not boil.

Transfer to a slow cooker to serve as an appetizer or serve over noodles as a meal.

Meat Loaf

This meat loaf is super easy. It goes great with cheesy potatoes (see page 118) and your favorite vegetable.

SERVES **6**

- 2 pounds ground beef
- 2 eggs
- 1½ cups bread crumbs
- ½ cup ketchup
- ½ cup water
- 1 package onion soup mix
- 4 strips bacon

Preheat oven to 350°F.

In a medium bowl, mix all the ingredients except bacon.

Place mixture in a 9 x 5-inch loaf pan.

Cover the top of the loaf with bacon. Bake for 1 hour.

Spaghetti Pie

This has all the flavor of lasagna, but it's a lot easier to make.

SERVES **6**

- 7 ounces spaghetti
- 2 tablespoons butter
- 1 cup Parmesan cheese
- 2 eggs, beaten
- 1 cup ricotta cheese
- 8 ounces shredded mozzarella cheese
- 1 pound sausage or ground beef
- ½ cup chopped onion
- 1 clove garlic, minced
- 1 (32-ounce) jar of your favorite spaghetti sauce
- Freshly grated Romano (optional)

Preheat oven to 350°F.

Cook spaghetti according to the package instructions; drain. Stir in butter.

Mix Parmesan cheese and beaten eggs. Stir into spaghetti.

Place in a 10-inch deep-dish pie plate.

Spread ricotta cheese on top of spaghetti.

Bake for 30 minutes. Remove from oven and cover with mozzarella cheese and put back in oven until the cheese is melted.

While cheese is melting, brown meat with garlic and onion. Add sauce and heat through.

Remove pie from oven and cut into wedges. Serve with meat sauce. Top with freshly grated Romano if desired.

Upside-Down Pizza

I got this recipe from my sister, Judy. It was my nephews' favorite when they were growing up.

SERVES APPROXIMATELY **6–8**

- 1 pound ground beef or sausage
- Italian seasoning, to taste
- Garlic powder, to taste
- 1 large jar pizza sauce
- 1 (12-ounce) package shredded mozzarella cheese
- 1 can crescent rolls

OPTIONAL

Mushrooms, fresh mozzarella, olives, peppers, onions, pepperoni, ham

Preheat oven to 400°F.

Brown ground beef or sausage; drain off grease and season with Italian seasoning and garlic powder.

Mix in pizza sauce and spread mixture in 9 x 13-inch pan.

Customize by adding your favorite pizza toppings over the meat sauce.

Cover toppings and meat sauce with cheese.

Unroll crescent roll dough and lay on top of cheese.

Bake about 10 minutes or until crescent rolls are golden brown.

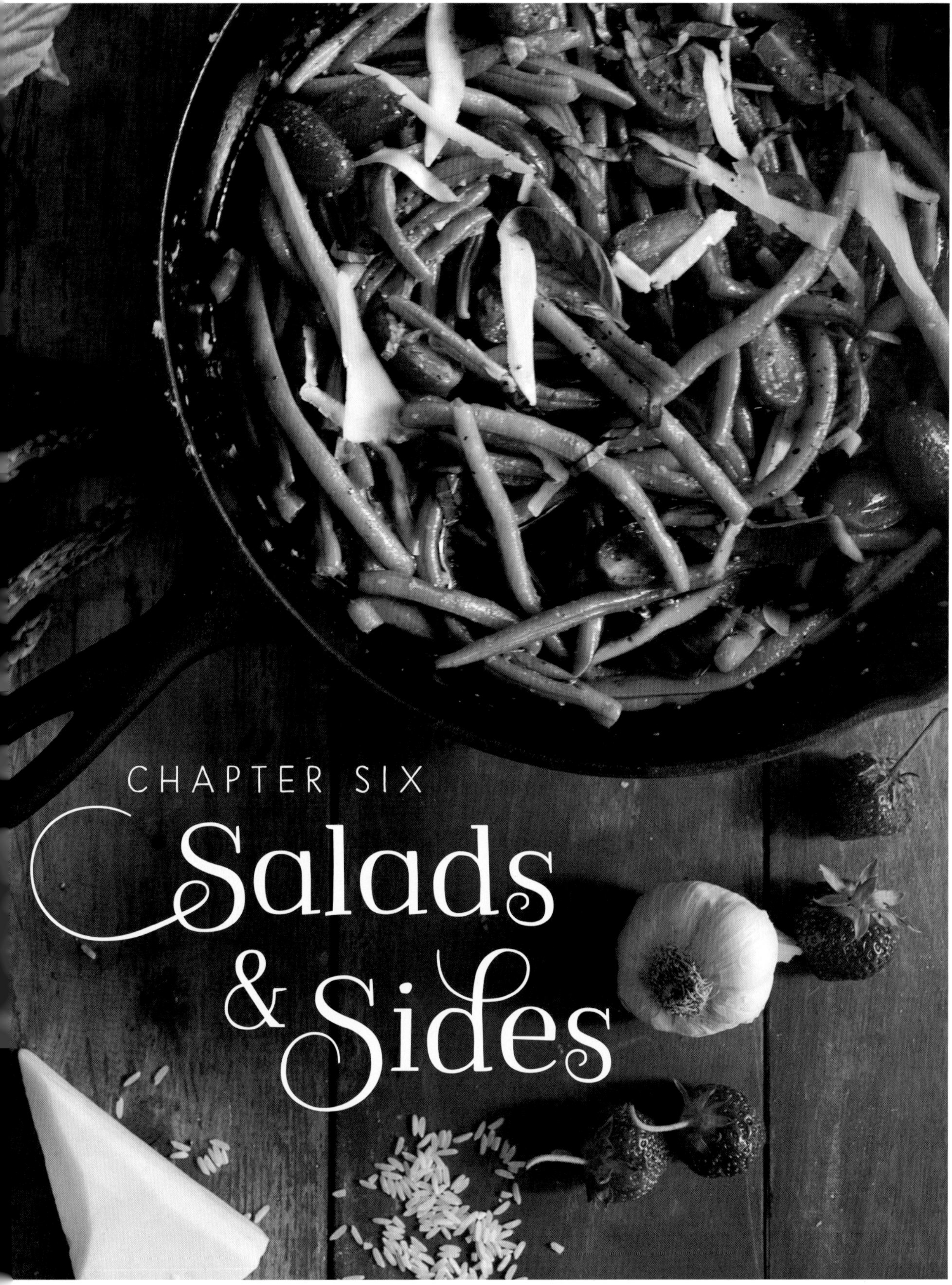

CHAPTER SIX

Salads & Sides

French Dressing

This thick, creamy dressing is quick and easy to make and is very tasty. I got the recipe many years ago from my Aunt Coke.

MAKES ABOUT 1½ CUPS

- ½ cup vegetable oil
- ¼ cup vinegar
- ⅓ cup ketchup or chili sauce
- ⅔ cup sugar
- 2 tablespoons lemon juice
- ½ teaspoon salt
- 1 tablespoon minced onion
- ½ teaspoon celery seed

Put all the ingredients in a tightly sealed container and shake.

Store in an airtight jar in the refrigerator for up to a month.

Strawberry Walnut Salad with Poppyseed Dressing

When I make this salad, I make individual salads so the pretty stuff stays on top. Serve with poppyseed dressing.

SERVES **6**

- 2 bunches of romaine lettuce, chopped
- 2 cups strawberries, halved or quartered depending on size of berries
- 1½ cups blueberries
- 4 ounces crumbled bleu cheese or feta cheese
- 1 package honey-roasted walnuts

Divide chopped lettuce into six bowls. Top with berries and cheese and nuts. Serve with poppyseed dressing.

Poppyseed Dressing

- ¾ cup oil
- ½ cup sugar
- ¼ cup vinegar
- ½ teaspoon dry mustard
- ½ teaspoon onion powder
- ½ teaspoon garlic powder
- 1 tablespoon poppy seeds
- Dash seasoned salt
- ½ teaspoon dry cilantro

Whisk ingredients together until mixed.

Serve immediately or store in the a sealed jar for up to a month in the refrigerator. Shake before using.

Make-Ahead Layered Chicken Salad

This salad is so delicious and looks pretty in a trifle dish. You can make it the night before if you want an easy side dish to bring to a picnic or potluck.

SERVES **10**

SALAD

1 ½ cups uncooked small shell pasta
1 tablespoon olive oil
3 cups shredded lettuce
4 hard-boiled eggs, chopped
½ teaspoon salt
¼ teaspoon pepper
3 cups cooked, diced chicken
2 cups frozen peas, thawed
1 tablespoon finely chopped onion
1 cup shredded mild cheddar cheese

DRESSING

1 cup mayonnaise
½ cup Henri's Tas-Tee dressing

Cook pasta according to package directions until tender. Drain and drizzle with olive oil.

Put lettuce in glass serving bowl; top with cooled pasta.

Spread chopped eggs over pasta and season with salt and pepper.

Layer on diced chicken, peas, and onion.

Mix dressing ingredients and spread on top.

Sprinkle on cheese.

Cover and refrigerate several hours or over night.

NOTE: *If you can't find Henri's Tas-Tee dressing in your local store, Marzetti's Original Slaw Dressing is a good alternative.*

Pasta Asparagus Salad

This is my favorite pasta salad. The asparagus and pine nuts add so much flavor.

SERVES **10** AS A SIDE

- ¾ pound spaghetti
- 2 pounds fresh asparagus, cut up
- 2 cups cherry tomatoes, halved
- ½ cup pine nuts
- Salt and pepper
- ¼ cup chopped onion
- 1 cup poppyseed dressing (see page 102)

Cook spaghetti in boiling salted water until almost done then add asparagus pieces and cook until asparagus is crisp and tender and spaghetti is done.

Drain, rinse in cold water, and drain again.

Pour into a serving bowl and add tomatoes, pine nuts, onion, salt and pepper.

Put on dressing and serve.

Meme's M-50-Drive-In Potato Salad

This was my Aunt Meme's recipe, which she served in our family restaurant back in the 1960s. When I would help her make it, she always instructed me to cut everything tiny. It was listed on of our menu as a side item and cost 20 cents.

SERVES **8**

6 large eggs
8 large potatoes
1 cup finely chopped celery
1 medium onion, chopped fine
1½ cups mayonnaise
1 tablespoon mustard
¼ cup pickle relish
1 tablespoon sugar
Salt and pepper to taste

OPTIONAL GARNISH

2 hard-boiled eggs, sliced

Place six eggs (eight if you want the optional garnish) in the bottom of a saucepan and cover with cold water. Heat the pot on high until boiling. Remove the pan from heat and cover. Let stand in hot water for 16 minutes. Then place in a bowl with ice water to cool.

Boil potatoes in salt water until tender, drain, cool, and chop.

Peel and chop six hard-boiled eggs. Mix eggs, celery, onion, and potatoes in a bowl. Add salt and pepper to taste. In separate bowl, mix mayonnaise, mustard, relish, and sugar. Pour onto potato mixture and combine.

If using garnish, slice the two reaming eggs and place them around the top of the salad.

Arborio Rice with Asparagus

I love to bring this side dish to potlucks—it's always a big hit.

SERVES **6**

1 medium onion, chopped
2 tablespoons olive oil
2 tablespoons butter
1 cup uncooked Arborio rice
3 cups chicken broth
1 pound asparagus, cut in ½-inch pieces

Cook onion in olive oil and butter for about 3 minutes.

Stir in rice and stir for 2 minutes.

Add one cup broth and cook, stirring, until liquid is absorbed.

Repeat with second cup of broth.

Then add third cup of broth and asparagus.

Cook until rice and asparagus are done.

If asparagus isn't quite done when liquid is absorbed, you can add more broth and cook a little longer.

BBQ Onions

Here is a tasty dish to bring to a tailgate party or a cookout.

SERVES **10**

- 11-ounce bag barbecue potato chips
- 2 (10½-ounce) cans cream chicken soup
- ½ cup whole milk
- 4 large sweet onions, sliced thin
- 2 cups shredded cheddar cheese

Preheat oven to 350°F.

Crush 2 cups of potato chips and set aside.

Stir together soup and milk.

Place ½ sliced onions in bottom of 9x13-inch pan that has been coated with vegetable spray.

Put a layer of uncrushed chips over onions, put 1 cup cheese over chips, and then ½ the soup mixture.

Repeat layers. Top with crushed chips.

Bake uncovered for 1 hour and 15 minutes.

DETROIT
PISTONS

Barb's Green Rice

Sometimes a dish becomes such a tradition that we relate it to the person who made it. My amazing sister-in-law, Barb, always brought this dish to Thanksgiving. We lost Barb much too soon. Now Barb's daughter, Betsy, whips this up for family gatherings. It's a popular side with a dash of nostalgia.

1½ cups Minute Rice
½ cups melted butter
2 cup broccoli, chopped
½ cup diced onion
1 (8-ounce) jar Cheez Whiz
1 (10½-ounce) can cream mushroom soup

SERVES **8**

Preheat oven to 350°F

In a medium bowl, mix all ingredients. Spread evenly in 9 x 13-inch baking dish.

Bake for 35 minutes.

Cauliflower & Cheese Sauce

Cheese makes cauliflower even better. This is a nice addition to a family meal.

1 stick butter
3/4 cup flour
1 teaspoon salt
3 cups milk
1/3 pound Velveeta cheese
1 medium-sized head cauliflower

SERVES **6**

In a medium saucepan over medium-heat, melt butter. Whisk in flour and salt until dissolved.

Add milk and cook until thick.

Add cheese and stir 1 minute or until cheese is melted and combined. Keep warm over low heat.

Trim any green stems off whole cauliflower.

Pour a half cup of water in the bottom of a covered casserole dish. Place cauliflower in dish and microwave for about 8 minutes or until fork tender.

Put cauliflower on a pretty plate and pour cheese sauce over the top. Serve immediately.

Cheesy Potatoes

I love to bring this dish to potlucks and cookouts. It goes great with so many main dishes, and it's always a hit.

SERVES **8**

1 (32-ounce) bag frozen potato cubes
1 (10½-ounce) can cream of mushroom soup
8 ounces shredded cheddar cheese
½ onion, chopped
1 cup sour cream
½ cup melted butter
½ cup whole milk

Preheat oven 350°F.

In a large bowl mix all ingredients and put in greased 9 x 13-inch pan.

Bake for 1 hour.

Slow Cooker Creamed Corn

This easy, make-ahead dish is perfect for a gathering or Sunday dinner.

2 (16-ounce) bags frozen yellow and white corn
1 (8-ounce) package cream cheese
1 stick butter
½ cup whole milk or half-and-half
2 tablespoons sugar
Salt and pepper to taste

SERVES **10**

Put all ingredients in slow cooker and cook on high for 3 hours.

Corn Cake

This easy corn cake adds a sweet complement to Mexican dishes. I use a mini ice cream scoop to serve up small portions.

SERVES **8**

- 1 (8½-ounce) box Jiffy corn muffin mix
- 1 (14¾ ounce) can cream style corn
- ½ cup butter
- 1 egg
- ⅓ cup sugar

Preheat oven to 375°F. Spray a loaf pan with nonstick cooking spray.

In a medium bowl, mix ingredients and pour in prepared pan.

Bake for 20 to 25 minutes.

Honeyed Carrots

I first had these carrots at a restaurant in Grayling, Michigan. I asked about the recipe and it was a simple one.

SERVES **8**

- 1 pound carrots
- 2 tablespoons butter
- 2 tablespoons honey

Prepare carrots by peeling and cutting them in diagonal pieces.

Cook over medium-high heat in salted water until tender.

Drain and add butter and honey; heat over medium heat for 3 to 4 minutes and serve.

Green Beans

With all the flavor of an Italian dish, these green beans make eating your veggies easy!

2 pounds fresh green beans
¼ cup salted butter
2 cloves garlic, minced
½ teaspoon salt
¼ teaspoon pepper
2 cups cherry tomatoes, halved
10–12 fresh basil leaves
Romano cheese (optional)

SERVES **8**

Boil beans in water until almost cooked to the doneness you prefer. Drain and set aside.

In skillet, melt butter over medium heat. Add garlic, salt, pepper, and tomatoes. Cook for about 3 minutes.

Add the beans to the skillet and stir gently so the tomatoes will not get crushed. Cook for an additional 3 to 4 minutes until hot throughout. Remove from heat.

Stack the basil leaves on top of each other. Cut ribbons of basil with kitchen shears directly onto the bean mixture. Stir gently and serve in skillet. Using a potato peeler, cut ribbons of Romano cheese to complete dish, if using.

Refried Beans

This recipe for refried beans is so good, you will never want to have canned beans again. It is a lot more work than opening a can but well worth the effort. I recommend doubling or tripling the recipe and freezing in small containers.

1 pound dry pinto beans
4 cups beef broth
2 onions, diced
2 cloves garlic, minced
1 bay leaf
1 teaspoon cumin
1 tablespoon chili powder
¾ cup butter
1 teaspoon salt
½ teaspoon pepper

SERVES **8**

Wash beans and put in large pot, then cover with water.

Bring to boil and simmer 3 minutes. Turn heat off and cover and let soak 3 hours.

Turn heat back on and simmer, covered, for 1 hour. Add water if necessary to keep beans covered.

Drain and rinse. Return to pot and add beef broth, one of the onions, one of the garlic cloves, bay leaf, cumin, and chili powder.

Bring to boil, lower heat, and simmer, leaving the cover slightly ajar, stirring occasionally, until the beans are tender, about 1½ hours.

When done, remove bay leaf.

Heat butter in a large skillet, add remaining onion and garlic, and cook until tender.

Purée 3 cups of the beans along with some liquid.

Add purée to skillet and cook to a thick paste.

Mash the remaining beans with a potato masher and add to skillet with the puréed beans.

Stir in salt and pepper.

LEVI'S
PICK

Macaroni and Cheese

This is the recipe I used when my kids were growing up. Now I make it for my grandkids.

SERVES **8**

1 pound box of pasta
3½ cups whole milk
8 ounces Velveeta cheese
1 cup grated mild cheddar cheese
¼ cup butter
Salt and pepper to taste

In a medium pot, cook pasta in salted water according to package instructions. Drain.

Add milk, cheeses, butter, and salt and pepper. Cook over medium heat until cheese is melted and everything is well blended. Add more milk if it needs to be a little more moist. Serve.

CHAPTER SEVEN

Cookies & Bars

Aunt Margaret's Sugar Cookies

This was my Great Aunt Margaret's recipe. My cousin Leah is the best at making them. Roll out dough very thin, and they will be melt-in-your-mouth delicious.

- 2 cups sugar
- ¾ cup butter
- ¾ cup shortening
- 2 eggs
- 1 teaspoon vanilla extract
- 4 tablespoons hot water
- 1 teaspoon baking soda
- 4½ cups flour

MAKES **5** DOZEN

Cream sugar, butter, shortening, and eggs; add vanilla.

Put baking soda in the hot water and add to mixture.

Mix in flour.

Cool in refrigerator for a few hours.

Roll out as thin as possible, then cut in desired shapes.

Bake at 400°F for 5 minutes.

Ma's Chocolate Chip Cookies

These were a big part of growing up at our house. They were the only cookies I remember my mom making.

MAKES ABOUT **4** DOZEN

1 cup shortening
¾ cup brown sugar
¾ cup white sugar
2 eggs
1 teaspoon baking soda
1 teaspoon hot water
2 cups flour
1 teaspoon salt
1 teaspoon vanilla extract
12 ounces semisweet chocolate chips

Preheat oven to 350°F.

Cream shortening, sugars, and eggs.

Dissolve baking soda in hot water and add to shortening mixture.

Mix in flour, salt, and vanilla.

Fold in chocolate chips.

Drop spoonfuls on cookie sheet.

Bake for 12 minutes or until golden brown.

Brownies

My mom made these brownies often and we all loved them. They are moist and delicious.

SERVES **18**

- 4 eggs
- 2 cups sugar
- 1 cup butter
- 6 tablespoons cocoa
- 2 teaspoons vanilla extract
- 1 cup flour
- ½ teaspoon salt
- 1 teaspoon baking powder
- 1 cup bittersweet baking chips, melted and cooled (optional)

Preheat oven 350°F. Grease a 9 x 13-inch pan.

In a medium bowl, cream eggs, sugar, butter, and vanilla.

In a separate bowl, combine dry ingredients. Sift the dry ingredients into the butter mixture.

Place in prepared pan.

Bake for 30 minutes. Don't overbake.

NOTE: *I think these brownies are just right as they are, but my daugher adds 1 cup of melted bittersweet (60% cacao) chocolate to the batter before baking.*

Rhubarb Bars

Enjoy these bars in the summer when the rhubarb is in season.

SERVES **18**

FILLING

3½ cups chopped rhubarb
1½ cups sugar
2 tablespoons cornstarch
¼ cup water
1 teaspoon vanilla extract

CRUST

1½ cups oatmeal
1½ cups flour
1 cup brown sugar
½ teaspoon baking soda
1 cup butter, softened
½ cup walnuts (optional)

Preheat oven to 350°F.

In a medium saucepan, cook filling ingredients until thick. Allow to cool.

Mix crust ingredients; put three quarters of the mixture in bottom of 9 x 13-inch pan. Press flat.

Spread the rhubarb mixture over crust.

Sprinkle remaining crust mixture over filling.

Bake for 25 minutes or until golden brown.

Dutch Butter Bars

These simple bars are so good they'll keep calling you back for another one.

MAKES **18**

1 cup butter
2 cups brown sugar
1 cup sugar
4 eggs
2 cups flour
1 teaspoon baking powder
½ teaspoon salt
1 teaspoon vanilla extract

Preheat oven to 350°F.

Mix butter, sugars, and eggs well. Add vanilla and dry ingredients.

Put in a greased 9 x 13-inch pan.

Bake for 30 minutes or until a toothpick comes out clean.

Blonde Brownies

Blonde brownies are the perfect combination of a chewy brownie and a chocolate chip cookie.

SERVES **18**

- ⅓ cup butter
- ⅓ cup shortening
- 2 cups brown sugar
- 2 eggs
- 2 teaspoons vanilla extract
- 2 cups flour
- 1 teaspoon baking powder
- ¼ teaspoon baking soda
- 1 teaspoon salt
- 6 ounces semisweet chocolate chips

Preheat oven to 350°F.

Place butter and shortening in saucepan and melt.

Stir in brown sugar, eggs, and vanilla.

Mix well and slowly add flour, baking powder, baking soda, and salt. Mix well after each addition.

Place in greased and floured 9 x 13-inch pan.

Sprinkle chocolate chips over top.

Bake for 35 minutes. Do not overbake.

Almond Bars

My friend Janet, from church, shared this recipe with me; when she brings these bars to our dessert auction, they always fetch a great price.

MAKES **15**

CRUST

½ cup butter
½ cup sugar
¼ teaspoon salt
1 egg plus 1 yolk (save the white)
1 cup flour

FILLING

1 cup sugar
1 cup almond paste
Juice of ½ lemon
2 eggs, separated
2 teaspoons sugar
1 teaspoon vanilla extract
1 cup sweetened, shredded coconut
1 cup chopped pecans (optional)

Preheat oven to 400°F.

Mix crust ingredients and press into a 9 x 13-inch pan.

Bake 10 minutes. Take out of oven and lower heat to 350°F.

Mix sugar, almond paste, lemon juice, and egg yolks. Beat until well blended.

Beat 3 egg whites until fluffy, add 2 teaspoons sugar and vanilla.

Fold egg whites into sugar paste mixture and pour over crust.

Sprinkle with coconut and nuts (if using).

Bake for 20 minutes.

Cool and cut into bars.

1/4 CUP

CHAPTER EIGHT

Cakes

Apple Cake

A wonderful fall weather cake. The warm sauce served over each piece when served takes this cake over the top with flavor.

SERVES **12–15**

CAKE

4 cups peeled, chopped apples
2 cups sugar
2 cups flour
1½ teaspoons baking soda
2 teaspoons cinnamon
1 teaspoon salt
2 eggs
¼ cup oil
2 teaspoons vanilla extract
1 cup chopped pecans

SAUCE TO SERVE OVER CAKE

1 stick butter
1 cup sugar
½ cup evaporated milk
1 teaspoon vanilla extract

To make the cake: Preheat oven to 350°F.

Mix apples, sugar, flour, baking soda, cinnamon, and salt and set aside.

Beat eggs, oil, vanilla, and pecans.

Mix with the apple mixture.

Pour in 9 x 13-inch greased pan and bake for 50 minutes.

To make the sauce: Boil this mixture for a few minutes.

Serve over each piece of warm cake, not the whole cake.

Banana Cake

If you have bananas that need to be used, try this recipe. Not only is it delicious, it will make your kitchen smell wonderful while baking.

SERVES **10**

GLAZE

⅓ cup butter
1 cup brown sugar
1 large banana, sliced

CAKE

⅓ cup shortening
2 eggs
1¼ cups sugar
1¾ cups mashed very ripe bananas
½ cup buttermilk
1 tablespoon vanilla extract
1½ cups flour
¾ teaspoon baking soda
½ teaspoon baking powder
½ teaspoon salt

Preheat oven to 325°F. Grease and flour a tube pan.

To make the glaze: Melt butter and combine with brown sugar.

Pour into prepared pan and arrange banana slices in glaze.

To make the cake: In a medium bowl, using a hand mixer, beat together shortening, eggs, sugar, bananas, buttermilk, and vanilla.

In a small bowl whisk together flour, baking soda, baking powder, and salt. Add flour mixture to shortening mixture. Beat until well combined.

Pour batter over brown sugar glaze in tube pan.

Bake for 1 hour or until center tests done.

Turn out of pan onto serving plate. Cool and serve.

Carrot Pineapple Cake

You won't even notice the pineapple in this cake, but it is an essential ingredient that makes it extra moist and amazing.

SERVES **12**

CAKE

4 eggs
1½ cups vegetable oil
2 cups cake flour
2 cups sugar
2 teaspoons cinnamon
2 teaspoons baking powder
2 teaspoons baking soda
1 teaspoon salt
2 cups grated carrots
1 cup crushed pineapple
1 tablespoon vanilla extract

CREAM CHEESE FROSTING

½ cup butter
1 (8-ounce) package cream cheese
1 pound powdered sugar
1 teaspoon vanilla extract
1 cup chopped walnuts

Preheat oven 350°F. Grease and flour two round 9-inch cake pans

To make the cake: Beat eggs and add oil and set aside.

Mix dry ingredients and stir into eggs-oil mixture.

Add carrots, pineapple, and vanilla; beat well.

Put into prepared pans.

Bake for 30 minutes or until toothpick comes out clean.

To make the frosting: beat cream cheese and butter until fluffy.

Add powdered sugar and vanilla and blend well.

Frost cooled cake and top with chopped walnuts.

Wedding Pound Cake

This was a favorite when I made wedding cakes. It's dense enough to be a pound cake, but light enough to work as a layer cake. Try it out for any celebration.

SERVES **12**

1 cup butter
½ cup shortening, plus more for the pans
3 cups sugar
5 eggs
3 cups flour, plus more for the pans
½ teaspoon baking powder
¼ teaspoon salt
1 cup milk
1 teaspoon lemon flavoring
1 teaspoon vanilla extract
Decorator frosting (page 154)
Raspberry filling (page 154)

Preheat oven to 325°F. Grease and flour two 9-inch round pans.

In a stand mixer with paddle attachment, mix butter and shortening. Add sugar and mix until completely combined.

Add eggs one at a time, beating after each one.

In a small bowl, mix flour, baking powder, and salt.

Add flour mixture to butter mixture, alternating with milk.

Add vanilla and lemon flavoring. Beat until well combined.

Bake for 1 hour or until toothpick comes out clean. Don't overbake.

Fill with raspberry filling and frost with decorator frosting.

Decorator Frosting

I used this recipe when I had my cake decorating business. It's a great consistency for piping and holds up better to temperature changes than butter-based recipes.

COVERS **1** 9-INCH, 2-LAYER CAKE

1½ cups shortening
1 teaspoon salt
3 tablespoons dry Dream Whip
1 tablespoon clear vanilla extract
1 teaspoon butter flavoring
1 teaspoon almond flavoring
2 pounds powdered sugar
½ cup water

In a stand mixer, beat the shortening, salt, Dream Whip, and flavorings for 2 minutes.

Add powdered sugar and water alternately.

Beat on high speed until fluffy.

Raspberry Filling

1½ cups frozen raspberries
1 tablespoon cornstarch
2 tablespoons lemon juice
¼ cup sugar

Combine in saucepan; cook over medium-high heat. Bring to a boil until mixture thickens.

Allow to cool completely before spreading onto cake.

Rum Cake

This was always a big hit in our hospitality room at National Guard Conferences.

SERVES **12**

CAKE

1 package Duncan Hines Butter Golden cake mix
1 package instant vanilla pudding
4 eggs
½ cup water
½ cup rum
½ cup vegetable oil
½ cup chopped pecans

GLAZE

¼ cup butter
¾ cup sugar
¼ cup rum
½ cup water

Preheat oven to 325°F. Spray a Bundt pan with nonstick spray.

Using a stand or hand mixer, beat all cake ingredients except pecans.

Sprinkle chopped pecans in bottom of prepared pan and pour batter on top.

Bake for 50 to 60 minutes.

Cool a few minutes and then turn out onto a plate.

In a medium saucepan, bring glaze ingredients to a boil. Allow to cool for a few minutes and then spoon slowly over cooled cake. The glaze should absorb into the cake.

CHAPTER NINE

Desserts

Apple Crisp

This fragrant fall dessert is an easy, delicious way to use the spoils of autumn.

SERVES **12**

- 6 large Granny Smith apples
- ¾ cup sugar
- ¾ tablespoon cinnamon
- 2 sticks butter
- 1½ cups flour
- ¾ cup brown sugar
- ¾ cup oatmeal
- 1 teaspoon baking powder

Preheat oven to 350°F.

Peel and slice apples and put in 9 x 13-inch pan sprayed with nonstick spray.

Mix sugar and cinnamon and sprinkle over apples.

Cut flour, brown sugar, oatmeal, and baking powder into butter.

Spread over apples and bake for 1 hour.

Serve warm with vanilla ice cream.

Dutch Apple Flat Pie

This is a nice variation of apple pie that makes a beautiful addition to a shower or family gathering. You can save the extra caramel sauce for ice cream.

SERVES **8–12**

Single pastry crust (page 183)

APPLE MIXTURE

⅔ cup sugar

3 tablespoons flour

1 teaspoon cinnamon

4 medium apples, peeled and diced

TOPPING

½ cup flour

⅓ cup packed brown sugar

½ cup oatmeal

1 teaspoon cinnamon

¼ cup butter (cold)

DRIZZLE

½ cup caramel topping (recipe follows)

Preheat oven to 350°F. Roll pastry to fit a 12-inch pizza pan. Fold under edges to give the pie a bit of a raised crust.

To make the apple mixture: combine sugar, flour, and cinnamon in a medium bowl. Add apples and toss. Arrange the apples in a single layer over the crust.

To make the topping: Cut the butter into small pieces and combine with the other topping ingredients. Mix with a fork or pastry blender to form a crumb. Do not overmix. Sprinkle topping evenly over apples.

Bake for 35 to 40 minutes or until apples are tender. Drizzle caramel while still hot. Cut into pieces and serve warm with ice cream.

Caramel Sauce

3 cups brown sugar

1½ cups light corn syrup

½ stick butter

1 (12-ounce) can evaporated milk

Mix brown sugar, corn syrup, and butter in saucepan and bring to a rolling boil. Remove from heat and let cool to room temperature. Add evaporated milk and mix well.

Fruit Pizza

This fruit pizza is a beautiful tasty dessert. The colors are flexible with the kind of fruit you use. If you don't have time to make the crust from scartch, you can use a roll of sugar cookie dough.

SERVES **12**

CRUST

¾ cup butter

½ cup powdered sugar

1½ cups flour

FILLING

1 (12-ounce) package of white chocolate baking chips

¼ cup cream

1 (8 ounce) package cream cheese

Assorted fruit

GLAZE

⅓ cup sugar

1½ tablespoons cornstarch

¾ cup fruit juice (pineapple, apple, or orange)

½ teaspoon lemon juice

Crust: Preheat oven to 325°F. Cream together butter and powdered sugar, blend in flour and press onto 12-inch pizza pan. Bake for 20 minutes until lightly browned. Cool completely.

Filling: Melt white chocolate in cream over low heat. Beat in cream cheese until smooth. Spread on cooled crust and chill. After chilled, put on assorted fruit.

Glaze: Combine sugar and cornstarch in small saucepan. Stir in juice and cook until thickened, stirring constantly. Drizzle cooled glaze over fruit.

Ice Cream Dessert

This has been a favorite of our family for a long time. I use my homemade fudge sauce on this dessert.

SERVES **12**

- 1 cup brown sugar
- 1 stick butter
- 1 teaspoon vanilla extract
- 2½ cups Rice Krispies
- ½ gallon vanilla ice cream
- Fudge sauce (recipe follows)

Bring brown sugar, butter, and vanilla to a good boil. Take off burner and add Rice Krispies. Press three quarters of Krispies in a 9 x 13-inch pan or Tupperware container.

Press ice cream over Rice Krispies. I like to put a little more ice cream than the half gallon but it's not necessary.

Spread chocolate fudge on ice cream.

Sprinkle remaining Rice Krispies on top.

Fudge Sauce

- 1 (12-ounce) can evaporated milk
- 1 pound powdered sugar
- 1 stick butter
- 3 squares unsweetened chocolate
- 1 teaspoon vanilla extract

Mix all ingredients in a double boiler and cook over hot water until it thickens, about 30 minutes. You will have leftovers that you can use on ice cream. Store extra in airtight container in refrigerator for up to four weeks.

Chocolate Chip Cookie Dough Cheesecake

This rich cheesecake is perfect for chocolate lovers and will be a hit and your next family gathering.

SERVES **12–15**

CRUST

2½ cups Oreo cookie crumbs

¼ cup melted butter

FILLING

3 (8-ounce) packages cream cheese

1 cup sugar

1 cup sour cream

2 teaspoons vanilla extract

3 eggs

COOKIE DOUGH

⅓ cup butter

¼ cup sugar

⅓ cup brown sugar

1 teaspoon vanilla extract

½ cup flour

1¾ cup mini chocolate chips, divided

Preheat oven to 350°F. Grease a 10-inch springform pan.

To make the crust: Mix Oreo cookie crumbs and melted butter. Spread on bottom and partially up the side of the prepared pan.

To make the filling: Beat softened cream cheese and sugar. Add sour cream and vanilla. Beat until smooth and then beat in eggs. Pour over crust.

To make the cookie dough: Cream softened butter and sugars and beat in vanilla. Add flour and mix well. Stir in ¾ cup mini chips.

Drop spoonfuls of cookie dough around on filling. Push dough into filling until completely covered. Set pan on a cookie sheet. Bake for 50 minutes or until center is about set. Run a knife around the edge of pan to loosen. Cool for 1 hour and then cover and refrigerate overnight.

Carefully remove side of pan and sprinkle 1 cup mini chips over top.

Oreo Cookie Dessert

This is a great dessert for chocolate lovers.

SERVES **12**

- 1 package Oreo cookies
- 1 stick melted butter
- 8 ounces cream cheese
- 1 cup powdered sugar
- 1 (12-ounce) tub Cool Whip
- 2 packages chocolate instant pudding, prepared

Crush cookies and mix with melted butter. Pat in 9 x 13-inch pan. Save some crumbs for top.

Mix cream cheese and powdered sugar and fold in Cool Whip. Spread on crust.

Mix pudding according to directions on box and spread on white layer.

Sprinkle remaining crumbs on top.

Joan's Strawberry Shortcake

You can do shortcake two ways, and I love them both. My friend Joan makes a biscuit-like shortcake that pairs beautifully with summer strawberries.

SERVES **6**

SHORTCAKE

2 cups flour
4 teaspoons baking powder
¼ cup sugar
½ teaspoon salt
¾ cup milk
1 egg
¼ cup butter

TOPPING

1 quart strawberries, hulled
⅓ cup sugar
Whipped cream

To make the shortcake: Preheat oven to 375°F. Grease an 8-inch square pan or a 6-jumbo-muffin pan.

Mix dry ingredients.

In another bowl whisk egg and milk together. Melt butter and whisk into milk and egg mixture.

Blend into dry ingredients.

Place in prepared pan.

Bake 20 minutes.

To prepare the berries: In a medium bowl, mix berries and sugar. Smash the berries with a potato masher. Allow to rest for about 30 minutes so the sugar completely dissolves.

To assemble: Cut warm shortcakes in two or three slices. Layer berries mixture and whipped cream over the shortcake and repeat.

Karen's Strawberry Shortcake

My friend Karen makes a sweet, cake-like shortcake. It's a different from the more typical biscuit-like shortcake, and it's just as good.

SERVES **6**

SHORTCAKE

2 cups flour
1 cup sugar
Dash of salt
3 teaspoons baking powder
½ cup butter
2 eggs
Milk

TOPPING

1 quart strawberries, hulled
⅓ cup sugar
Whipped cream

To make the shortcake: Preheat oven to 350°F. Grease a 9-inch square pan.

Mix dry ingredients and cut in cold butter until crumbly.

In a 2-cup measuring cup, beat 2 eggs, add milk to make 1⅓ cups, and then blend together.

Blend liquid into dry ingredients.

Bake for 20 to 30 minutes.

To prepare the berries: In a medium bowl mix berries and sugar. Smash the berries with a potato masher. Allow to rest for about 30 minutes so the sugar completely dissolves.

To serve: Top individual pieces of the shortcake with berry mixture and whipped cream.

Crunch Bar Ice Cream Dessert

This make-ahead dessert hits the spot on a hot summer day, and will be loved by chocolate and peanut butter fans.

6 Crunch candy bars, crushed
1 cup peanut butter
2 cups graham cracker crumbs
¾ gallon vanilla ice cream, softened
Smucker's Chocolate Magic Shell

SERVES **12**

Break candy bars into small pieces with a rolling pin or food processor.

Mix with peanut butter and cracker crumbs.

Pat two thirds of this mixture into 9 x 13-inch pan.

Add ice cream and then the remaining crumb mixture and top with Magic Shell.

Freeze and serve after the chocolate is set. Store in an airtight container in the freezer for up to two weeks.

Peach Enchiladas

This is an easy, quick, and yummy dessert. Serve with vanilla ice cream or whipped cream.

SERVES **10**

- 2 packages crescent rolls
- 4 large, fresh peaches, peeled, pitted, and quartered
- 1 cup sugar
- 1 cup butter
- 1 teaspoon cinnamon
- 1 can Mountain Dew soda

Preheat oven to 350°F. Coat a 9 x 13-inch pan with nonstick spray.

Unroll crescent rolls and separate into triangles.

Put one peach quarter on each triangle, roll up, and place in pan.

In small bowl, combine sugar, melted butter, and cinnamon. Spoon over rolls.

Pour soda on top.

Bake for 45 minutes.

Serve hot.

CHAPTER TEN
Pies

Grammy Vonk's Pie Crust

This old recipe is from my Grandma Vonk. She handed it down to my Aunt Meme, who used it to make all the pie crusts for the cream pies for our restaurant.

1 cup flour
1 teaspoon salt
2 heaping tablespoons lard
3 tablespoons water

MAKES **1** CRUST

Combine flour and salt. Cut lard into the flour. Add water. Press together and roll out on a floured surface.

No-Roll Pie Crust

If you don't like rolling pie dough or you're not too good at it, like me, try this one. It's easy and tastes great. I use it for the cream pies in this book (see page 185).

1½ cups flour
½ teaspoon salt
2 tablespoons sugar
2 tablespoons milk
½ cup oil

MAKES **1** CRUST

Preheat oven to 400°F.

Mix dry ingredients and add oil and milk. Mix well and pat into a 9-inch pie plate.

Bake for 10 minutes.

Cream Pie Four Ways

This is a yummy recipe for a few different cream pie variations. I use the no-roll pie crust recipe in this book (see page 183).

SERVES **8**

- 1 (9-inch) baked pie crust
- ⅔ cup sugar
- ½ teaspoon salt
- 4 tablespoons cornstarch
- 3 cups milk
- 4 egg yolks
- 2 tablespoons butter
- 1½ teaspoons vanilla extract

Stir together sugar, salt, and cornstarch in a saucepan. Blend milk and egg yolks together and stir into sugar mixture.

Cook over medium heat, stirring constantly, until mixture boils and thickens. Boil 1 minute, blend in butter and vanilla.

Coconut cream pie: Add ¾ cup sweetened flaked coconut to cream mixture. Pour into prepared crust. Lay plastic wrap on filling and chill in refrigerator 3 to 4 hours. Serve with whipped cream and toasted coconut on top. (Brown ¼ cup coconut in a little melted butter.)

Banana cream pie: Pour half the filling in prepared crust and then add a layer of sliced bananas and the rest of filling. Lay plastic wrap on filling and refrigerate 3 to 4 hours. Serve with whipped cream.

Cherry cream pie: Pour filling in crust and when it's cooled, spread cherry pie filling on top. Serve with whipped cream.

Chocolate peanut butter cream pie: As soon as filling is cooked add ¼ cup creamy peanut butter and ¾ cup chocolate chips. Stir until chips are melted and pour into prepared crust. Chill in refrigerator for 3 to 4 hours. Serve with whipped cream.

Dutch Apple Pie

When apple season is here, bake up this sweet, buttery Dutch Apple pie.

SERVES **8**

1 (9-inch) unbaked pie crust

FILLING

2/3 cup sugar

2 tablespoons flour

1 teaspoon cinnamon

4 1/2 cups peeled and sliced Granny Smith apples

1 tablespoon lemon juice

CRUMB TOPPING

1 cup flour

3/4 cup quick oats

1/2 cup brown sugar

1/2 teaspoon cinnamon

3/4 cup butter

Preheat oven to 375°F.

To make the filling: Combine first 4 ingredients and sprinkle over apples and stir. Add lemon juice and stir. Spoon into crust.

To make the topping: Mix all ingredients until blended and crumbly.

Sprinkle over apple mixture. Bake 45 minutes.

Serve warm with vanilla ice cream.

Chocolate Chip Cookie Pie

This rich pie is will please chocolate-lovers. It makes a nice addition to a pie spread on Thanksgiving.

SERVES **8**

1 (9-inch) unbaked pie crust
¾ cup butter, softened
½ cup sugar
½ cup brown sugar
2 eggs
1 tablespoon vanilla extract
½ cup flour
1 cup chocolate chips
¾ cup chopped nuts (optional)

Preheat oven to 325°F.

With a mixer, beat together butter and sugars for 1 to 2 minutes.

Mix in eggs, vanilla, and flour.

Stir in chocolate chips and nuts (if using).

Pour into pie crust and bake for 55 minutes or until knife comes out clean.

Serve warm with ice cream or whipped cream.

Peach Pie

Nothing says summer like warm peach pie. Your guests will be thrilled, and your house will smell amazing when you bake this pie.

SERVES **8**

- 1 egg white
- 1 (9-inch) unbaked pie crust
- ¾ cup flour
- ½ cup packed brown sugar
- ⅓ cup sugar
- ¼ cup cold butter
- 6 cups peeled and sliced fresh peaches

Preheat oven to 375°F.

Beat egg white until foamy; brush over bottom and sides of the crust.

In a bowl, combine flour and sugars; cut in butter until mixture resembles fine crumbs. Sprinkle two thirds of mixture in bottom of crust.

Top with peaches and sprinkle with remaining crumb mixture.

Bake for 40 to 45 minutes until filling is bubbly and peaches are tender.

Pecan Joy Pie

With a pie this rich, you might need an extra cup of coffee.

SERVES **10**

1 (9-inch) unbaked pie crust
3 beaten eggs
1 cup light corn syrup
⅓ cup sugar
⅓ cup brown sugar
⅓ cup melted butter
¼ teaspoon salt
1 teaspoon vanilla extract
1 cup milk chocolate chips
1 cup sweetened flaked coconut
1 cup coarsely chopped pecans
Whipped cream (optional)

Preheat oven to 350°F.

Mix eggs, corn syrup, sugar, brown sugar, butter, salt, and vanilla.

In bottom of unbaked crust, layer chocolate chips, coconut, and pecans.

Pour filling mixture over chocolate mixture, spread evenly.

Bake 50 minutes or until center looks like it's set when you shake the pie gently.

Serve warm with whipped cream.

Rhubarb Pie

My neighbor grew rhubarb in her backyard, and I love to bake with this perennial, tart vegetable whenever it's in season.

SERVES **8**

- 2 (9-inch) unbaked pie crusts
- 2 eggs
- 1½ cups sugar
- 4 tablespoons flour
- 4 cups rhubarb, diced
- 2 tablespoons butter

Preheat oven to 375°F.

Beat eggs slightly and stir in sugar and flour. Mix in rhubarb and put in pastry-lined pie plate.

Cut butter into small pieces. Dot the top of the rhubarb with butter.

To make lattice top: Using a pizza cutter, cut the second crust into 1-inch strips. Space half of the dough strips evenly across the top of the pie. Fold back alternating strips and place a new strip perpendicular to the original strips. Unfold the bottom strips to their original position. Repeat this step, alternating the strips that you fold back, to create a basket weave effect. Trim dough that hangs over the edge of the pie and pinch top lattice crust to the bottom crust.

Bake for 50 to 60 minutes.

Pumpkin Pie

The cream cheese makes this recipe stand out from your typical pumpkin pie.

SERVES **8**

- 1 (9-inch) unbaked pie crust
- 1 (8-ounce) package cream cheese, softened
- 2 cups canned pumpkin
- 1 cup sugar
- ¼ teaspoon salt
- 1 egg + 2 egg yolks beaten
- 1 cup half-and-half
- ¼ stick butter melted
- 1 teaspoon vanilla extract
- ¾ teaspoon cinnamon

Preheat oven to 350°F.

Put crust in pie plate and cover with foil. Put pie weights on and bake 10 minutes. Remove pie weights and foil and bake 10 more minutes.

To make the filling: Beat cream cheese and pumpkin, add sugar and salt and beat. Add egg, yolks, half-and-half, and butter; beat.

Then add vanilla and cinnamon. Beat until well blended.

Bake 1 hour or until a knife comes out clean when inserted in center of pie.

Serve with whipped cream.

Strawberry or Peach Pie

This is wonderful fresh strawberry pie that is refreshing and cool on a hot summer day.

SERVES **8**

CRUST

½ cup butter
1 cup flour
1 tablespoon sugar
1 tablespoon water

FILLING

1 cup sugar
2 rounded tablespoons cornstarch
Pinch of salt
1 cup water
3 tablespoons strawberry Jell-O
1 quart hulled, sliced strawberries
Cool Whip

Preheat oven to 350°F.

Mix crust ingredients and pat in pie pan. Bake 20 minutes. Cool.

Mix sugar, cornstarch, salt, and water in a medium saucepan. Cook over medium heat until thick and clear. Add Jell-O. Cool.

Add strawberries to cooled Jell-O mixture and pour into cooled crust. Refrigerate for 3 to 4 hours before serving.

To serve: Top with Cool Whip and garnish with whole strawberries.

To make peach pie: Use peach Jell-O and replace strawberries with peeled, sliced peaches.

CHAPTER ELEVEN

Merry Christmas

Brickle Graham Bites

If you love toffee, these treats will make a super-sweet addition to your holiday parties or get-togethers.

SERVES **24**

- 20 whole graham crackers
- 1 cup butter, melted
- 1 cup sugar
- 1 beaten egg
- ¼ cup milk
- ½ cup graham cracker crumbs
- ½ cup Heath Bits O' Brickle

FROSTING

- ½ stick butter, softened
- 2 cups powdered sugar
- 1 teaspoon vanilla extract
- 1 tablespoon whole milk (plus more if needed)

Mix butter, sugar, egg, and milk in a medium saucepan. Cook over medium-high heat, stirring constantly, until mixture boils. Remove from heat and allow to cool to room temperature.

Add graham crackers crumbs and brickle bits.

Cover the bottom of a 9 x 13-inch pan with whole graham crackers. Pour butter and sugar mixture over the crackers and top with a second layer of graham crackers.

Mix frosting ingredients and spread on top graham crackers. Sprinkle more brickle bits on top of frosting.

Cover and refrigerate overnight

Cut in small bars.

Pecan Pie Bars

These bars are like bite-sized pecan pie. They are perfect for any holiday party spread.

SERVES **18**

CRUST

1¾ cups flour
¾ cup butter, softened
⅓ cup sugar
⅓ cup coarsely chopped pecans

FILLING

1½ cups corn syrup
⅔ cup firmly packed dark brown sugar
4 large eggs
6 tablespoons flour
2 teaspoons vanilla extract
1 teaspoon salt
1½ cups coarsely chopped pecans

Preheat oven to 350°F.

To make the crust: In a medium bowl with a pastry blender, cut together flour, butter, and sugar. Stir in pecans.

Press crust mixture evenly into a 13 x 9-inch pan. Bake for 20 minutes or until edges are light golden brown.

To make the filling: Combine all filling ingredients except pecans in bowl; mix well. Stir in pecans. Spread evenly over hot, partially baked crust. Bake 30 to 35 minutes or until filling is set. Cool completely. Cut into squares.

Fast and Easy Fudge

Try this fudge recipe if you're short on time and don't want to mess with a candy thermometer.

2 sticks butter, plus more for the pan
5 cups sugar
1 (12-ounce) can evaporated milk
6 ounces semisweet chocolate chips
12 ounces milk chocolate chips
10 ounces marshmallow cream
2 cups chopped, roasted walnuts (optional)

SERVES **30**

Butter a 9 x 13-inch pan and set aside.

In a large pot, cook butter, sugar, and milk over medium heat. When mixture reaches a boil, continue cooking for 8 minutes, continuously stirring.

Add the rest of the ingredients and stir until chocolate is completely melted and marshmallow cream is completely combined.

Pour into prepared pan. Allow to cool completely before cutting.

NOTE: *For thinner fudge, replace 9x13-inch pan with a jelly-roll pan.*

Graham Cracker Cookies

I ordered some amazing-sounding cookies one year, and when they arrived, I was surprised that they were exactly like these cookies, which I'd been making for years.

SERVES **60**

- 15 whole graham crackers, broken into quarters
- 2 sticks butter
- ½ cup chopped pecans
- ½ cup sugar
- 3 ounces milk chocolate chips (optional)

Preheat oven to 350°F.

Line a jelly-roll pan with parchment paper. Place graham crackers on paper. Fit crackers as close together as possible.

Sprinkle the pecans on crackers and set aside.

In a medium saucepan, bring the butter and sugar to a boil. Spoon the mixture over crackers.

Bake for 10 minutes.

If using chocolate chips, sprinkle on top while hot. When the chocolate softens, spread it over the tops of the crackers.

Place cookie sheet in refrigerator to harden chocolate.

When chocolate has set, lift cracker cookies off the foil and break apart.

Peanut Butter Fudge

My sister-in-law Barb made this at Christmas and it brings back fond memories of our family gatherings.

6 cups sugar
3 cups milk
17 ounces peanut butter
13-ounce jar marshmallow cream

SERVES **50**

Line a jelly-roll pan with parchment paper.

Clip a candy thermometer to the side of a large pot. Cook sugar and milk until it reaches 245°F.

Add peanut butter and marshmallow cream. Pour onto prepared jelly-roll pan.

When fudge cools, lift the fudge out of the pan using the parchment paper and cut into small pieces.

Kettle Corn

I know throwing a bag of popcorn in the microwave is so easy, but this is so much better. This salty sweet treat makes a great addition to your party table.

MAKES **12** CUPS

2 tablespoons vegetable oil
2 tablespoons butter
½ cup popping corn
3 tablespoons sugar
½ teaspoon salt

Heat oil and butter in large saucepan at medium-high heat.

Add popping corn, sprinkle sugar evenly over popping corn, and place lid on pan.

When it starts to pop, shake the pan back and forth to prevent burning.

When popping slows, remove from burner and set cover ajar to let out the steam.

When popping stops, uncover and sprinkle on salt.

Kettle Corn
PAGE 211
Party Mix
PAGE 214

White Chocolate Party Mix PAGE 215

Party Mix

This is always part of our Christmas celebrations. I created this version; it has the perfect amount of butter and is so much better than the original.

SERVES **25**

- 6 cups Cheerios
- 6 cups Rice Chex
- 6 cups Corn Chex
- 6 cups thin pretzels
- 1 pound mixed nuts
- 6 cups Bugles
- 1½ cups butter
- ½ cup vegetable oil
- 2 tablespoons Worcestershire sauce
- 1 teaspoon onion salt
- 1 teaspoon garlic salt

Preheat oven to 250°F.

Mix cereals, pretzels, nuts, and Bugles in an extra large roasting pan.

In a medium saucepan, melt butter and add oil, Worcestershire sauce, onion salt, and garlic salt. Whisk together and cook until salts are completely dissolved.

Pour evenly over cereal mixture and mix well.

Bake for 1 hour, stirring every 15 minutes.

Store in an airtight container for up to two weeks.

White Chocolate Party Mix

For a sweet twist on party mix, try this super easy recipe. Pour some in a pretty bowl for any holiday gathering.

SERVES **15**

- 3 cups pretzels
- 3 cups Bugles
- 3 cups Rice Chex
- 1½ cups red and green M&M's
- 12 ounces white chocolate

Mix pretzels, Bugles, Rice Chex, and M&M's in a large bowl.

Melt chocolate in a double boiler until creamy.

Pour over pretzel mixture.

Stir until it's evenly covered.

Spread on cookie sheet. When cool and set, break into pieces.

Store in airtight container for up to two weeks.

Peanut Brittle

This peanut brittle is a tradition at our house. I used to give it to my kids' teachers for a Christmas gift every year. It won a blue ribbon at the Hudsonville Fair many years ago. You have to have a little patience cooking this candy, as it takes a while to reach 300°F.

SERVES **20**

- 2 cups sugar
- 1 cup light corn syrup
- ½ cup water
- 2 sticks butter + more for the cookie sheet
- 2 cups Spanish peanuts
- 1 teaspoon baking soda

Butter 2 cookie sheets and set aside.

Clip a candy thermometer to a large saucepan.

Mix sugar, corn syrup, and water in the saucepan and cook over medium heat. When it starts to boil, add butter.

Boil at medium heat, stirring constantly. When the mixture reaches 280°F, add peanuts.

Adding the peanuts cools the mixture and it takes awhile for the temperature go back up. Stir constantly until temperature reaches 300°F.

Take off burner and add baking soda.

Mix well and pour onto the prepared cookie sheets. Spread by shaking pans side to side. Some air bubbles should remain.

Cool completely.

Break into pieces and store in an airtight container for up to two weeks.

Peanut Butter Balls

If you like to get your kids or grandkids involved in the kitchen, this is a great time to call them in to help. Little hands are excellent at mixing the dough and forming the peanut butter balls. These are hands down the family favorite; it just wouldn't be Christmas without them.

1 cup butter
1 (16-ounce) jar of creamy peanut butter
1 pound powdered sugar
3½ cups Rice Krispies
8-ounce Hershey bar
12 ounces semisweet chocolate chips
1–2 tablespoons vegetable shortening (optional)

MAKES ABOUT **50**

Line two cookie sheets with parchment or foil and set aside.

Melt butter and mix with peanut butter, powdered sugar, and Rice Krispies in a large bowl.

Form into balls and place on prepared cookie sheets.

In a double boiler, melt chocolates. If chocolate is too thick you can add 1 to 2 tablespoons of shortening to thin it.

Using two forks, dip each ball in chocolate. Allow excess chocolate to run off before placing the ball back onto the cookie sheet.

Refrigerate until chocolate is set. If you have any extra chocolate, you can drizzle it over the set chocolate.

After drizzled chocolate is set, move balls to an airtight container and store in refrigerator for up to 2 weeks.

CHAPTER TWELVE

Canning & Freezing

How to Can

WHAT YOU'LL NEED:

A canning pot or other large pot with lid

Glass jars (such as Ball), new lids, and rings

Jar lifter

Clean kitchen towels

Fill your canning pot half full with water. Start heating water over medium heat.

Jars and rings can be reused many times, but lids should be new each time you can. Check jars for chips or cracks on rim, and discard any that do not have a perfect rim. Wash jars and lids in hot, soapy water; rinse. Place clean jars in the hot water bath in the canning pot to keep them hot. Lids and rings should be dried and set aside on a clean towel.

Food should be canned while it is still hot. Take a hot jar out of the water with jar lifter and fill with hot food. Leave approximately 1 inch of headspace at top of jar. Wipe jar rims with a clean, damp cloth. Put lid on and and screw ring on tightly. Return jar to the canning pot. Repeat with all jars until all the food is in jars. Add enough water to cover jars by one inch. Place lid on canning pot and bring water to boil. Process in boiling water for the time specified in the recipe.

After processing, turn off heat, remove pot lid, and let jars stand in canning pot for 10 minutes.

Remove jars from canning pot with jar lifter. Set on a towel to cool. Allow jars to rest for 12 to 24 hours. Check all seals by pressing on center of lid. If the center of the lid pops back up when you press it, the lid did not seal. Refrigerate any jars that did not seal and use within the next few days. Place sealed jars in a cool dark place, and store for up to 18 months.

For more information on canning, visit freshpreserving.com.

Burrito Sauce

The chilies pack this sauce with amazing flavor. I use it for burritos but it's also great on enchiladas.

12 mild dried chili pods (such as Anaheim)
1 large sweet onion, chopped
2 teaspoons salt
1½ tablespoons cumin
3 teaspoons chili powder
2 garlic cloves, minced
3 cups water
¾ cup cooking oil
1 gallon tomato sauce

MAKES 5½ PINTS

Soak chili pods in water until completely soft.

Remove stems and seeds.

Place in a blender with the onion, salt, cumin, chili powder, garlic, and water. Blend until puréed.

In large saucepan over medium-high heat, add oil. When oil is hot, add contents of blender and stir until blended. Be careful, as this mixture can spatter.

Add tomato sauce and simmer 3 minutes.

Pack in hot sterile jars with hot lids and put rings on tightly. Process in canning bath for 20 minutes. See "How to Can" on page 224.

Stewed Tomatoes

Here's a way to preserve a little bit of summer in your pantry. Can these when your local tomatoes are in season. They are handy for all your recipes that call for stewed tomatoes. I use mine in homemade goulash (see page 74).

16 cups peeled, cored, quartered tomatoes
2 green peppers
2 orange peppers
2 yellow peppers
2 red peppers
3 large onions
1 bunch of celery
2 tablespoons salt
2 cups vinegar
⅔ cup white sugar
⅔ cup brown sugar
½ cup cold water
3 tablespoons cornstarch

Wash, peel, core, and quarter tomatoes and put in large pot.

Core and destem peppers. Peel outer layer of onions and cut into quarters. Remove the white portion of celery stalk and discard. Cut stalks into 2 to 3-inch pieces. Wash peppers, onions, and celery and place in a food processor. Chop fine.

Add the chopped vegetables to tomatoes. Add salt, vinegar, and sugars. Bring to a boil and simmer 1½ hours. Stir often to prevent sticking to bottom of pan.

Mix water and cornstarch and stir into tomato mixture. Boil a few minutes until it thickens. Pack in hot sterile jars with hot lids and put rings on tightly. Process in canning bath for 20 minutes. See "How to Can" on page 224.

Tomato Soup
PAGE 231
Salsa
PAGE 232

Sweet Zuccinni Relish
PAGE 230
Burrito Sauce
PAGE 225

Sweet Zucchini Relish

Put your garden-fresh zucchini to good use.

MAKES ABOUT **6** PINTS

FIRST DAY

8–10 medium zucchinis
4 cups onion, chopped finely
1 red pepper, chopped finely
1 green pepper, chopped finely
5 tablespoons canning salt

SECOND DAY

2½ cups white vinegar
6 cups sugar
3 tablespoons cornstarch
1 teaspoon dry mustard
¾ teaspoon nutmeg
¾ teaspoon turmeric
1½ teaspoons celery seed
½ teaspoon pepper

First day: Chop first-day ingredients in food processor. Be careful to not over process. Put this mixture in a glass covered bowl. Refrigerate overnight.

Second day: In a large pot, combine all second-day ingredients and bring to a boil.

Rinse zucchini mixture in cold water and drain well in a sieve. Add veggie mixture to the boiling vinegar mixture. Cook on medium for 30 minutes. Put hot mixture into 6 hot sterile pint jars or 12 sterile half-pint jars. Put hot lids on and tighten lids. Process in hot water bath for 15 minutes. See "How to Can" on page 224.

Tomato Soup

I decided to try making a quick version of the tomato soup I've been canning for years using V8 juice instead of going to all the work of cooking the tomatoes and vegetables. This turned out really tasty and was quick to make.

MAKES **6** PINTS

- 2 (64-ounce) bottles of V8 juice
- $\frac{2}{3}$ cup flour
- $\frac{1}{4}$ cup brown sugar
- 1 teaspoon salt
- $\frac{1}{2}$ cup butter

Pour V8 juice in large pot.

Take about 2 cups of the juice and put in a bowl. Add the flour, sugar, and salt to the juice to the bowl.

Whisk these ingredients until well blended.

Add this mixture to the pot. Whisk together and bring to a boil. Cook until thick.

Add the butter.

When butter is melted and blended, cook for 2 more minutes.

Pack in hot sterile pint jars with hot lids and put rings on tightly. Process in canning bath for 20 minutes. See "How to Can" on page 224.

Salsa

A great salsa for all your Mexican dishes, and for omelettes and scrambled eggs too.

MAKES **10** PINTS

- 1 gallon diced tomatoes
- 3 jalapeño peppers, diced
- 4 large onions, diced
- 4 green peppers, diced
- 2 yellow peppers, diced
- 2 (12-ounce) cans tomato paste
- ¾ cup sugar
- 1 cup white vinegar
- 3 teaspoons canning salt
- 1 tablespoon garlic powder
- 1 tablespoon onion powder

When dicing jalapeños, discard seeds for a mild salsa, keep for spicy salsa.

Place all ingredients in a large pot and cook on medium-low for 2 to 3 hours.

Pack in hot sterile jars with hot lids and put rings on tightly. Process in canning bath for 20 minutes. See "How to Can" on page 224.

Applesauce

Here's a delicious way to enjoy local apples year round.

MAKES 4 PINTS

3 pounds McIntosh apples
¾ cup water
⅓ cup sugar
½ teaspoon cinnamon

Peel, core, and slice apples.

Cook apples in ¾ cup water until apples are tender.

Mash apples with potato masher.

Add sugar and cinnamon.

Freezer Corn

Freezing corn is a family tradition. When you buy local in-season corn, you'll be able to later prepare corn far better than any store-bought frozen corn. We enjoy this all year and always include it at Thanksgiving. Get your kids or grandkids to help husk the corn.

9 cups corn
2 cups water
¼ cup sugar
1 teaspoon salt
Butter for serving

Husk corn. Using a sharp knife, cut corn off cob raw.

Put 9 cups corn in large pan; add water, sugar, and salt.

Bring to a boil, and boil for 2 minutes.

Pour into a flat pan to cool.

When cooled, place in freezer bags in amounts of your preference and freeze.

To reheat, place ¼ to ½ cup water in the bottom of a medium saucepan. Add frozen corn and cook covered on medium-low heat until corn is thawed. Increase heat to medium-high and cook uncovered until hot. Stir in butter to taste and serve immediately.

Freezer Strawberry Jam

Toast and peanut butter with strawberry jam. Fast breakfast. This recipe makes two 8-ounce containers. Can make up to 3 batches at a time.

1⅔ cups strawberries, cleaned and hulled
⅔ cup sugar
2 tablespoons Ball RealFruit Instant Pectin

MAKES **16** OUNCES

Hull and wash strawberries.

In a 9 x 13-inch pan crush strawberries with a potato masher.

Stir sugar and fruit pectin together in a medium bowl.

Add crushed strawberries to the sugar.

Stir by hand for 3 minutes.

Place in freezer containers.

Let stand 30 minutes. Freeze.

When you're ready to use the jam, move a jar from your freezer to your refrigerator.

Acknowledgments

This cookbook wouldn't have been possible without my book-designer daughter. From food styling to photography to rewrites and designs, Laura knew exactly what had to be done to make this book happen.

Leah, your help in the kitchen to tweak dishes and get them just right was indispensable. Thank you for proofing and sharing so much with me over the years.

Thank you to my many taste-testers who critiqued my recipes; some of which made the cut and some didn't. Pastor Rich, Linda, Carroll, and Sandi especially enjoyed this part of the process. I appreciate your honesty and encouragemtent.

Thanks to my grandkids: Joseph, Megan, Matthew, Levi, and Leo for choosing a favorite and taking part in a photo shoot. Thank you Betsy (and Sam) for sharing and being photographed with Barb's Green Rice.

I appreciate everyone who swapped recipe cards with me. All the church friends, Guard friends, family, and school buddies who shared their ideas, fellowship, and food. Your generosity, kindness, and love has meant the world to me.

Special thanks to Nicole Frail and Abigail Gehring at Skyhorse Publishing for believing in my book. Thank you to proofreader Mark Amundsen for your sharp attention to detail.

I am so grateful for the strong women and amazing cooks from my youth. Helene, Meme, and Barb; I wish you were here to celebrate this book with me. To my twin, Judy, thank you for waiting tables with me and sharing my love of cooking.

Thanks be to God for all these people and the patience to accomplish a lifelong dream.

Index

A

Almond Bars, 143
American Goulash, 74
Anaheim chilis
  Chili con Queso, 10
appetizers
  Asian Meatballs, 6
  Bleu Cheese Artichoke Appetizer, 8
  Chili con Queso, 10
  Guacamole Dip, 17
  Joy's Olive Spread, 13
  Veggie Pizza, 9
Apple Cake, 146
Apple Crisp, 160
apples
  Dutch Apple Flat Pie, 163
  Dutch Apple Pie, 186
Applesauce, 233
Arborio Rice with Asparagus, 110
artichoke hearts
  Bleu Cheese Artichoke Appetizer, 8
Asian Meatballs, 6
asparagus
  Arborio Rice with Asparagus, 110
  Creamed Asparagus on Biscuits, 89
  Pasta Asparagus Salad, 107
Aunt Margaret's Sugar Cookies, 131
avocado
  Crustless Avocado Quiche, 37
  Guacamole Dip, 17

B

bacon
  Creamy Slow Cooker Potato Soup, 51
  Meat Loaf, 92
  Sausage Egg and Cheese Breakfast Braid, 46
Baked French Toast, 38
Banana Bread, 22
Banana Cake, 148
barbecue sauce
  Caledonia Band Booster Chili, 60
Barb's Green Rice, 115
barley
  Beef, Beer, and Barley Soup, 65
BBQ Onions, 113
beans
  Caledonia Band Booster Chili, 60
  Refried Beans, 124
  Taco in the Round, 14
  Wet Burritos, 73
beef
  ground
    American Goulash, 74
    Caledonia Band Booster Chili, 60
    Dutch Meatball Soup, 63
    Meat Loaf, 92
    Pig in Blankets, 45
    Spaghetti Pie, 95
    Swedish Meatballs, 91
    Taco in the Round, 14
    Upside-Down Pizza, 97
    Wet Burritos, 73
Beef, Beer, and Barley Soup, 65
beef roast
  Beef, Beer, and Barley Soup, 65
Beer Bread, 25
bell peppers
  Salsa, 232
  Stewed Tomato, 227
  Sweet Zucchini Relish, 230
  biscuits
  Creamed Asparagus on Biscuits, 89
  Easy Biscuits, 26
Bleu Cheese Artichoke Appetizer, 8
Blonde Brownies, 140
blueberries
  Buttermilk Pancakes with Blueberry Sauce, 43
  Strawberry Walnut Salad with Poppyseed Dressing, 102
Blueberry Muffins, 29
bread crumbs
  Asian Meatballs, 6
  Meat Loaf, 92
Bread Machine Honey Oatmeal Bread, 30
breads
  Baked French Toast, 38
  Banana Bread, 22
  Beer Bread, 25
  Blueberry Muffins, 29
  Easy Biscuits, 26
  Six-Week Bran Muffins, 21
  Zucchini Bread, 33
Breakfast Pizza, 40
breakfasts
  Breakfast Pizza, 40
  Crustless Avocado Quiche, 37
  Pig in Blankets, 45
  Sausage Egg and Cheese Breakfast Braid, 46
Brickle Graham Bites, 203
broccoli
  Barb's Green Rice, 115
Broccoli Soup, 55
Brownies, 134
Bugles
  Party Mix, 214
  White Chocolate Party Mix, 215
burritos
  Wet Burritos, 73
burrito sauce
  Wet Burritos, 73
Burrito Sauce, 225
Buttermilk Pancakes with Blueberry Sauce, 43
Butternut Squash Soup, 59

C

cake
  Banana Cake, 148
  Carrot Pineapple Cake, 151
  Chocolate Chip Cookie Dough Cheesecake, 169
  Joan's Strawberry Shortcake, 172
  Karen's Strawberry Shortcake, 175
  Rum Cake, 157
  Wedding Pound Cake, 152
Caledonia Band Booster Chili, 60
canning, 224
caramel sauce, 163
Carrot Pineapple Cake, 151
carrots
  Beef, Beer, and Barley Soup, 65
  Broccoli Soup, 55
  Chicken Soup, 54
  Dutch Meatball Soup, 63
  Dutch Pea Soup, 50
  Honeyed Carrots, 122
  Potato Cheese Soup, 69
  Vegetable Beef Soup, 56
cauliflower
  Vegetable Cheese Soup, 67
Cauliflower & Cheese Sauce, 116
cheddar cheese soup
  Vegetable Cheese Soup, 67
Cheerios
  Party Mix, 214
cheese
  bleu
    Bleu Cheese Artichoke Appetizer, 8
    Strawberry Walnut Salad with Poppyseed Dressing, 102
  cheddar
    BBQ Onions, 113
    Cheesy Potatoes, 118
    Chicken Tater Tot Casserole, 83
    Macaroni and Cheese, 127
    Make-Ahead Layered Chicken Salad, 105
    Potato Cheese Soup, 69
    Taco in the Round, 14
    Tortilla Chicken Casserole, 84
  Colby
    Breakfast Pizza, 40
    Broccoli Soup, 55
    Creamy Slow Cooker Potato Soup, 51
    Veggie Pizza, 9
    Wet Burritos, 73
  cottage
    Taco in the Round, 14
  feta
    Strawberry Walnut Salad with Poppyseed Dressing, 102
  Monterey Jack

Chili con Queso, 10
mozzarella
Crustless Avocado Quiche, 37
Spaghetti Pie, 95
Upside-Down Pizza, 97
Parmesan
Breakfast Pizza, 40
Spaghetti Pie, 95
ricotta
Spaghetti Pie, 95
Romano
Green Beans, 123
Sausage Egg and Cheese Breakfast Braid, 46
Swiss
Swiss Cheese Chicken and Mushroom Bake, 76
Velveeta
Cauliflower & Cheese Sauce, 116
Chili con Queso, 10
Macaroni and Cheese, 127
Cheesy Potatoes, 118
Cheez Whiz
Barb's Green Rice, 115
Broccoli Soup, 55
chicken breast
Chicken Pot Pie, 79
Chicken Soup, 54
Chicken Tater Tot Casserole, 83
Leah's Chicken Squares, 80
Make-Ahead Layered Chicken Salad, 105
Swiss Cheese Chicken and Mushroom Bake, 76
Tortilla Chicken Casserole, 84
Chicken Pot Pie, 79
Chicken Soup, 54
Chicken Tater Tot Casserole, 83
Chili con Queso, 10
chocolate bar
Peanut Butter Balls, 217
Chocolate Chip Cookie Dough Cheesecake, 169
Chocolate Chip Cookie Pie, 189
chocolate chips
Blonde Brownies, 140
Chocolate Chip Cookie Dough Cheesecake, 169
Chocolate Chip Cookie Pie, 189
Fast and Easy Fudge, 206
Graham Cracker Cookies, 209
Ma's Chocolate Chip Cookies, 132
Peanut Butter Balls, 217
Pecan Joy Pie, 193
chocolate pudding
Oreo Cookie Dessert, 170
Christmas
Brickle Graham Bites, 203
Fast and Easy Fudge, 206
Graham Cracker Cookies, 209
Kettle Corn, 211
Party Mix, 214
Peanut Brittle, 217
Peanut Butter Balls, 218
Peanut Butter Fudge, 210
Pecan Pie Bars, 204
White Chocolate Party Mix, 215
cocoa
Brownies, 134
coconut
Almond Bars, 143
Pecan Joy Pie, 193
cookies
Aunt Margaret's Sugar Cookies, 131
Ma's Chocolate Chip Cookies, 132
Cool Whip
Oreo Cookie Dessert, 170
Strawberry or Peach Pie, 198
corn
Chicken Tater Tot Casserole, 83
Freezer Corn, 234
Kettle Corn, 211
Slow Cooker Creamed Corn, 119
Corn Cake, 120
Corn Chex
Party Mix, 214
Corn Dogs, 87
crackers
Chicken Tater Tot Casserole, 83
Dutch Meatball Soup, 63
cream cheese
Carrot Pineapple Cake, 151
Chocolate Chip Cookie Dough Cheesecake, 169
Creamy Slow Cooker Potato Soup, 51
Fruit Pizza, 164
Joy's Olive Spread, 13
Leah's Chicken Squares, 80
Oreo Cookie Dessert, 170
Pumpkin Pie, 197
Sausage Egg and Cheese Breakfast Braid, 46
Slow Cooker Creamed Corn, 119
Swedish Meatballs, 91
Taco in the Round, 14
Veggie Pizza, 9
Creamed Asparagus on Biscuits, 89
cream of chicken soup
BBQ Onions, 113
Chicken Tater Tot Casserole, 83
Swiss Cheese Chicken and Mushroom Bake, 76
Tortilla Chicken Casserole, 84
cream of mushroom soup
Barb's Green Rice, 115
Cheesy Potatoes, 118
Chicken Tater Tot Casserole, 83
Swedish Meatballs, 91
Swiss Cheese Chicken and Mushroom Bake, 76
Tortilla Chicken Casserole, 84
cream of potato soup
Chicken Pot Pie, 79
Cream Pie Four Ways, 185
Creamy Slow Cooker Potato Soup, 51
crescent rolls
Breakfast Pizza, 40
Leah's Chicken Squares, 80
Peach Enchiladas, 179
Sausage Egg and Cheese Breakfast Braid, 46
Upside-Down Pizza, 97
Veggie Pizza, 9
Crunch Bar Ice Cream Dessert, 176
Crustless Avocado Quiche, 37

D

Decorator Frosting, 154
desserts. *See also* cake; cookies; pies
Apple Crisp, 160
Chocolate Chip Cookie Dough Cheesecake, 169
Crunch Bar Ice Cream Dessert, 176
Dutch Apple Flat Pie, 163
Fruit Pizza, 164
Ice Cream Dessert, 164
Joan's Strawberry Shortcake, 172
Karen's Strawberry Shortcake, 175
Oreo Cookie Dessert, 170
Peach Enchiladas, 179
Dutch Apple Flat Pie, 163
Dutch Apple Pie, 186
Dutch Butter Bars, 138
Dutch Meatball Soup, 63
Dutch Pea Soup, 50

E

Easy Biscuits, 26
eggs
Breakfast Pizza, 40
Crustless Avocado Quiche, 37
Make-Ahead Layered Chicken Salad, 105
Meme's M-5-Drive-In Potato Salad, 108
Pig in Blankets, 45

F

Fast and Easy Fudge, 206
Freezer Corn, 234
Freezer Strawberry Jam, 236
French Dressing, 101
frosting, 154
Fruit Pizza, 164
fudge sauce, 164

G

Graham Cracker Cookies, 209
graham crackers
Brickle Graham Bites, 203
Crunch Bar Ice Cream Dessert, 176
Grammy Vonk's Pie Crust, 183
Green Beans, 123
green chilies
Tortilla Chicken Casserole, 84
green peppers
Salsa, 232
Stewed Tomato, 227
Sweet Zucchini Relish, 230
Guacamole Dip, 17

H

ham
Vegetable Cheese Soup, 67
Heath Bits O' Brickle, 203

honey
Bread Machine Honey Oatmeal Bread, 30
Butternut Squash Soup, 59
Honeyed Carrots, 122
Honeyed Carrots, 122
hot dogs
Corn Dogs, 84

I

ice cream
Crunch Bar Ice Cream Dessert, 176
Ice Cream Dessert, 164
Ice Cream Dessert, 166

J

jalapeño pepper
Salsa, 232
Jell-O
Strawberry or Peach Pie, 198
Joan's Strawberry Shortcake, 172
Joy's Olive Spread, 13

K

kale
Polish Kielbasa Slow Cooker Soup, 64
Karen's Strawberry Shortcake, 175
ketchup
French Dressing, 101
Meat Loaf, 92
Swedish Meatballs, 91
Kettle Corn, 211

L

Leah's Chicken Squares, 80
leeks
Dutch Meatball Soup, 63
lettuce
Make-Ahead Layered Chicken Salad, 105
Strawberry Walnut Salad with Poppyseed Dressing, 102
Taco in the Round, 14
Wet Burritos, 73

M

Macaroni and Cheese, 127
main dishes
American Goulash, 74
Chicken Pot Pie, 79
Chicken Tater Tot Casserole, 83
Corn Dogs, 84, 87
Creamed Asparagus on Biscuits, 89
Meat Loaf, 92
Spaghetti Pie, 95
Swiss Cheese Chicken and Mushroom Bake, 76
Tortilla Chicken Casserole, 84
Upside-Down Pizza, 97
Wet Burritos, 73
maple syrup
Baked French Toast, 38
marshmallow cream
Fast and Easy Fudge, 206
Peanut Butter Fudge, 210
Ma's Chocolate Chip Cookies, 132
mayonnaise
Joy's Olive Spread, 13
Make-Ahead Layered Chicken Salad, 105
Meme's M-5-Drive-In Potato Salad, 108
Veggie Pizza, 9
Meat Loaf, 92
Meme's M-5-Drive-In Potato Salad, 108
milk
Cream Pie Four Ways, 185
Sausage Egg and Cheese Breakfast Braid, 46
M&M's
White Chocolate Party Mix, 215
Mountain Dew soda
Peach Enchiladas, 179
muffins
Blueberry Muffins, 29
Six-Week Bran Muffins, 21
mushrooms
Swiss Cheese Chicken and Mushroom Bake, 76

N

noodles
American Goulash, 74
Dutch Meatball Soup, 63
Macaroni and Cheese, 127
Make-Ahead Layered Chicken Salad, 105
Pasta Asparagus Salad, 107
Spaghetti Pie, 95
Swedish Meatballs, 91
No-Roll Pie Crust, 183

O

oatmeal
Apple Crisp, 160
Dutch Apple Flat Pie, 163
Pig in Blankets, 45
Rhubarb Bars, 137
Swedish Meatballs, 91
olives
Joy's Olive Spread, 13
Tortilla Chicken Casserole, 84
onions
BBQ Onions, 113
onion soup mix
Meat Loaf, 92
orange peppers
Stewed Tomato, 227
Oreo Cookie Dessert, 170

P

Party Mix, 214
Pasta Asparagus Salad, 107
Peach Enchiladas, 179
peaches
Strawberry or Peach Pie, 198
Peach Pie, 190
Peanut Brittle, 217
peanut butter
Crunch Bar Ice Cream Dessert, 176
Peanut Butter Balls, 218
Peanut Butter Fudge, 210
peas
Dutch Pea Soup, 50
Make-Ahead Layered Chicken Salad, 105
Pecan Joy Pie, 193
Pecan Pie Bars, 204
pecans
Almond Bars, 143, 146
Graham Cracker Cookies, 209
Joy's Olive Spread, 13
Pecan Pie Bars, 204
Zucchini Bread, 33
pectin
Freezer Strawberry Jam, 236
pie crust
Chicken Pot Pie, 79
Grammy Vonk's Pie Crust, 183
No-Roll Pie Crust, 183
pies
Chocolate Chip Cookie Pie, 189
Cream Pie Four Ways, 185
Dutch Apple Pie, 186
Peach Pie, 190
Pecan Joy Pie, 193
Pumpkin Pie, 197
Rhubarb Pie, 194
Strawberry or Peach Pie, 198
Pig in Blankets, 45
pineapple
Carrot Pineapple Cake, 151
pine nuts
Pasta Asparagus Salad, 107
Polish Kielbasa Slow Cooker Soup, 64
popping corn
Kettle Corn, 211
Poppyseed Dressing, 102
Pasta Asparagus Salad, 107
Potato Cheese Soup, 69
potato chips
BBQ Onions, 113
potatoes
Breakfast Pizza, 40
Cheesy Potatoes, 118
Creamy Slow Cooker Potato Soup, 51
Dutch Pea Soup, 50
Meme's M-5-Drive-In Potato Salad, 108
Polish Kielbasa Slow Cooker Soup, 64
Potato Cheese Soup, 69
pretzels
Party Mix, 214
White Chocolate Party Mix, 215
pudding
Oreo Cookie Dessert, 170
Rum Cake, 157
pumpkin
Butternut Squash Soup, 59
Pumpkin Pie, 197

R

ranch dressing mix
Veggie Pizza, 9
Raspberry Filling, 154
red peppers
Stewed Tomato, 227
Sweet Zucchini Relish, 230
refried beans

Taco in the Round, 14
Refried Beans, 124
relish
Meme's M-5-Drive-In Potato Salad, 108
Sweet Zucchini Relish, 230
Rhubarb Bars, 137
Rhubarb Pie, 194
rice
Arborio Rice with Asparagus, 110
Barb's Green Rice, 115
Chicken Soup, 54
Dutch Meatball Soup, 63
Vegetable Beef Soup, 56
Rice Chex
Party Mix, 214
White Chocolate Party Mix, 215
Rice Krispies
Ice Cream Dessert, 164
Peanut Butter Balls, 217
Rum Cake, 157

S
salad dressings
French Dressing, 101
Poppyseed Dressing, 102
salads
Make-Ahead Layered Chicken Salad, 105
Meme's M-5-Drive-In Potato Salad, 108
Pasta Asparagus Salad, 107
Strawberry Walnut Salad with Poppyseed Dressing, 102
salsa, 232
Guacamole Dip, 17
Taco in the Round, 14
sausage
Breakfast Pizza, 40
Crustless Avocado Quiche, 37
Pig in Blankets, 45
Polish Kielbasa Slow Cooker Soup, 64
Sausage Egg and Cheese Breakfast Braid, 46
Upside-Down Pizza, 97
Sausage Egg and Cheese Breakfast Braid, 46
scallions
Asian Meatballs, 6
sides
Arborio Rice with Asparagus, 110
Barb's Green Rice, 115
BBQ Onions, 113
Green Beans, 123
Honeyed Carrots, 122
Macaroni and Cheese, 127
Six-Week Bran Muffins, 21
Slow Cooker Creamed Corn, 119
soups
Beef, Beer, and Barley Soup, 65
Broccoli Soup, 55
Butternut Squash Soup, 59
Caledonia Band Booster Chili, 60
Chicken Soup, 54
Creamy Slow Cooker Potato Soup, 51
Dutch Meatball Soup, 63
Dutch Pea Soup, 50
Polish Kielbasa Slow Cooker Soup, 64
Potato Cheese Soup, 69
Tomato Soup, 231
Vegetable Beef Soup, 56
sour cream
Banana Bread, 22
Blueberry Muffins, 29
Cheesy Potatoes, 118
Chocolate Chip Cookie Dough Cheesecake, 169
Guacamole Dip, 17
Taco in the Round, 14
Tortilla Chicken Casserole, 84
Wet Burritos, 73
soy sauce
Asian Meatballs, 6
Spaghetti Pie, 95
squash
Butternut Squash Soup, 59
Stewed Tomatoes, 227
strawberries
Freezer Strawberry Jam, 236
Joan's Strawberry Shortcake, 172
Karen's Strawberry Shortcake, 175
Strawberry Walnut Salad with Poppyseed Dressing, 102
Strawberry or Peach Pie, 198
Strawberry Walnut Salad with Poppyseed Dressing, 102
stuffing mix
Leah's Chicken Squares, 80
Swiss Cheese Chicken and Mushroom Bake, 76
Swedish Meatballs, 91
Sweet Zucchini Relish, 230
Swiss Cheese Chicken and Mushroom Bake, 76

T
Taco in the Round, 14
taco seasoning, 14
Taco in the Round, 14
Wet Burritos, 73
tater tots
Chicken Tater Tot Casserole, 83
teriyaki sauce, 6
Asian Meatballs, 6
tomatoes
American Goulash, 74
Caledonia Band Booster Chili, 60
Chili con Queso, 10
Green Beans, 123
Pasta Asparagus Salad, 107
Salsa, 232
Stewed Tomato, 227
Taco in the Round, 14
Vegetable Beef Soup, 56
Veggie Pizza, 9
tomato sauce
Burrito Sauce, 225
Spaghetti Pie, 95
Upside-Down Pizza, 97
tomato soup
American Goulash, 74
Tomato Soup, 231
Tortilla Chicken Casserole, 84
tortillas
Wet Burritos, 73
turkey
ground
Asian Meatballs, 6
Caledonia Band Booster Chili, 60

U
Upside-Down Pizza, 97

V
V8 juice
Tomato Soup, 231
vanilla ice cream
Crunch Bar Ice Cream Dessert, 176
Ice Cream Dessert, 164
vanilla pudding
Rum Cake, 157
Vegetable Beef Soup, 56
Vegetable Cheese Soup, 67
Veggie Pizza, 9

W
walnuts
Carrot Pineapple Cake, 151
Fast and Easy Fudge, 206
Rhubarb Bars, 137
Strawberry Walnut Salad with Poppyseed Dressing, 102
Zucchini Bread, 33
Wedding Pound Cake, 152
Wet Burritos, 73
white chocolate
White Chocolate Party Mix, 215
white chocolate chips
Fruit Pizza, 164
White Chocolate Party Mix, 215

Y
yellow peppers
Salsa, 232
Stewed Tomato, 227

Z
zucchini
Sweet Zucchini Relish, 230
Zucchini Bread, 33

Conversion Charts

METRIC AND IMPERIAL CONVERSIONS

(These conversions are rounded for convenience)

Ingredient	Cups/Tablespoons/ Teaspoons	Ounces	Grams/Milliliters
Butter	1 cup/16 tablespoons/ 2 sticks	8 ounces	230 grams
Cheese, shredded	1 cup	4 ounces	110 grams
Cornstarch	1 tablespoon	0.3 ounce	8 grams
Cream cheese	1 tablespoon	0.5 ounce	14.5 grams
Flour, all-purpose	1 cup/1 tablespoon	4.5 ounces/0.3 ounce	125 grams/8 grams
Flour, whole wheat	1 cup	4 ounces	120 grams
Fruit, dried	1 cup	4 ounces	120 grams
Fruits or veggies, chopped	1 cup	5 to 7 ounces	145 to 200 grams
Fruits or veggies, puréed	1 cup	8.5 ounces	245 grams
Honey, maple syrup, or corn syrup	1 tablespoon	0.75 ounce	20 grams
Liquids: cream, milk, water, or juice	1 cup	8 fluid ounces	240 milliliters
Oats	1 cup	5.5 ounces	150 grams
Salt	1 teaspoon	0.2 ounces	6 grams
Spices: cinnamon, cloves, ginger, or nutmeg (ground)	1 teaspoon	0.2 ounce	5 milliliters
Sugar, brown, firmly packed	1 cup	7 ounces	200 grams
Sugar, white	1 cup/1 tablespoon	7 ounces/0.5 ounce	200 grams/12.5 grams
Vanilla extract	1 teaspoon	0.2 ounce	4 grams

OVEN TEMPERATURES

Fahrenheit	Celsius	Gas Mark
225°	110°	¼
250°	120°	½
275°	140°	1
300°	150°	2
325°	160°	3
350°	180°	4
375°	190°	5
400°	200°	6
425°	220°	7
450°	230°	8

About the Author

JOYCE KLYNSTRA has loved cooking since her teenage years, which she spent working in a family-run, drive-in restaurant. She continued her passion for cooking with a wedding cake business, hosting church dinners, and working in hospitality with her Army husband. She takes joy in fellowship and food with the many loved ones she has acquired in her seventy-three years. She lives in Lansing, Michigan. This is her first book.